Caring for a blind cat

by Natasha Mitchell MVB CertVOphthal MRCVS

www.catprofessional.com

ISBN 978-0-9556913-1-7

About Cat Professional

Cat Professional was founded in 2007 by Dr Sarah Caney with the aims of providing cat owners and veterinary professionals with the highest quality information, advice, training and consultancy services.

Publications

Cat Professional is a leading provider of high quality publications on caring for cats with a variety of medical conditions. Written by international experts in their field, each book is written to be understood by cat owners and veterinary professionals. The books are available to buy through the website www.catprofessional.com as eBooks where they can be downloaded and read instantly. Alternatively they can be purchased as a softback via the website and specialist bookstores.

'*Caring for a blind cat*' is the second in a series of books published by Cat Professional. Forthcoming publications include:

- '*Caring for a cat with lower urinary tract disease*' – August 2008

- '*Caring for a hyperthyroid cat*' – September 2008

- '*Caring for a diabetic cat*' – November 2008

German and Japanese translations of each book will be made available.

A variety of free-to-download articles also feature on the Cat Professional website.

Advice, Training and Consultancy

Cat Professional is dedicated to improving the standards of cat care and in this capacity is a provider of Continuing Professional Development to veterinary surgeons and other professionals working with cats around the world.

Cat Professional also works closely with leading providers of cat products and foods providing training programmes, assisting with product literature and advising on product design and marketing.

Specialist feline medicine advice is available to veterinary professionals and cat owners world-wide. Details are available on the website.

About the author

Natasha Mitchell grew up in Co Tipperary, Ireland. She graduated from University College Dublin in 1998 with a degree in Veterinary Medicine. She spent one year working in a mixed practice in the UK, followed by three years working and travelling in Australia. It was there that she developed an interest in ophthalmology and started to study the subject. She returned to the UK to study for a Royal College of Veterinary Surgeons Certificate in Veterinary Ophthalmology which she obtained in 2004. She then worked in referral ophthalmology in Hampshire UK for 18 months followed by the Eye Veterinary Clinic in Herefordshire UK (www.eyevetclinic.co.uk). Recently she has returned to her homeland and is working as an ophthalmologist in Limerick, Ireland. Natasha has published articles in both UK and Irish veterinary journals, and in cat charity bulletins. She has conducted lectures to veterinarians and veterinary students in the UK and Ireland.

About this book

Natasha worked closely with Dr Sarah Caney who was running a Feline Clinic, and was inspired with a love for cats and feline medicine. She frequently deals with eye problems in cats, and was struck with the huge loss that some owners felt when their cats became blind. It was difficult to provide the help and support they needed within the confines of a consulting room, and Sarah encouraged Natasha to compile a guide for owners of blind cats to help them through the difficult times. This book is aimed at cat owners with blind or visually impaired cats, owners of cats with eye problems that may lead to blindness and at people thinking of re-homing a blind or disabled cat.

This book has been written as an electronic book available for downloading or printing on demand. If you have obtained this book free from a friend or another source I would encourage you to visit www.catprofessional.com to obtain a bona fide copy of your own.

Words in green are contained in the glossary section at the end of the book.

Acknowledgements

The author is very grateful to Dr Sarah Caney for the inspiration to write this book and for her dedication in wishing to better the lives of cats. The author is also very grateful to Liam and Melanie, Anette, Linda, Karen, Lynne and Dean for writing about their experiences with their blind cats, and providing photographs of them. Photographs were also provided by John Mould, Peter and Helen Gibson, Karen Dunn and the Blind Cat & Rescue Sanctuary, North Carolina USA.

CONTENTS

Eye problems in cats are not uncommon, and with prompt veterinary care many of these can be treated. However despite the best efforts of dedicated veterinarians, some eye conditions lead to irreversible blindness. It can be devastating to learn that your cat will not see again. It is a big change for both you and your cat. This book will guide you through those changes and help you to provide the very best for your cat so that they can still lead a happy and fulfilling life.

Important Legal Information:

Cat Professional Ltd has developed this book with reasonable skill and care to provide general information on feline health and care in relation to eye disease and blindness in cats. This book however does not, and cannot, provide advice on any individual situation. It is not a substitute for advice from a veterinary surgeon on each individual situation.

Cat Professional Ltd therefore strongly recommends that users seek, and follow, advice from their veterinary surgeon on any health or other care concerns that they may have concerning their cats. Users should not take, or omit to take, action concerning the health or care of their cats in reliance on the information contained in this book and so far as permissible by law, Cat Professional Ltd excludes all liability and responsibility for the consequences of any such action or omission in reliance on that information. While this book does not provide advice on, or recommend treatments or medications for, individual situations, users attention is brought to the fact that some of the medications referred to in this book may not be licensed (veterinary approved) in all countries and therefore may not be available in all countries.

Coping with the bad news

Hearing that a treasured companion has lost or is about to lose their sight is distressing news. It is normally very difficult to absorb the reasons behind these changes and to understand their implications within the confines of a clinical consulting room. Later on when you have both returned home, you have time to start to deal with your emotions and decide how best to move forward. We naturally grieve for something which is lost, and losing vision seems like a huge obstacle to overcome. Talking to loved ones and sympathetic friends is very important.

Cats with a visual disability usually lead very happy and fulfilling lives. It is important not to underestimate how incredibly adaptable they are. They can rapidly learn to live with blindness while maintaining a very good quality of life. Cats are far more adaptable than we humans are, and the change is often a lot harder for the owner than for the cat!

We must remember not to assume that the cat feels the same way about the situation as we do. Cats do not have the same emotions that we do, and life is much more straight-forward for them. They do not worry for the same reasons that we worry. A cat's requirements are very basic – all they require is food, water, shelter, a safe place to relieve themselves and social enrichment of their lives. Of course they also require a slave to do their bidding, and that has always been your job! What is devastating to us is not necessarily such a trauma for them. Time, understanding and patience will usually allow your cat to adapt smoothly.

Cats dislike changes when given the choice, but when such a situation is a reality for them, they have a remarkable ability to adapt without fuss. New limitations can only be learned by experience and then memorised. Behaviour changes will

> **Cats with a visual disability usually lead very happy and fulfilling lives. It is important not to underestimate how incredibly adaptable they are.**

occur but these can be positive. Small changes are required to accommodate a cat which cannot see. There are simple things that you can change around the home to make life more comfortable for them.

People will always ask many questions on hearing such bad news. Was this my fault? Was there something that I could have done to prevent this? Should I have brought my cat to the vet sooner? It is always difficult to answer those questions in retrospect. You are very unlikely to have personally caused your cat to go blind. Many of the conditions which cause blindness are not preventable. Genetic diseases cannot be halted, and infections can happen and be difficult to control. Occasionally vision could have been saved by bringing your cat to the vet earlier. For example with high blood pressure (hypertension), the early signs can be detected by an experienced veterinarian before retinal detachment occurs. However it is perfectly reasonable not to bring your cat to the veterinarian until the obvious signs of blood in the eye and blindness occur, by which time it may be too late to save vision. Cats frequently do not display signs of ill-health in an obvious manner, and it is hard to notice that they are sleeping more or less active. We can only do our best for them when we understand what is happening and move forward from there.

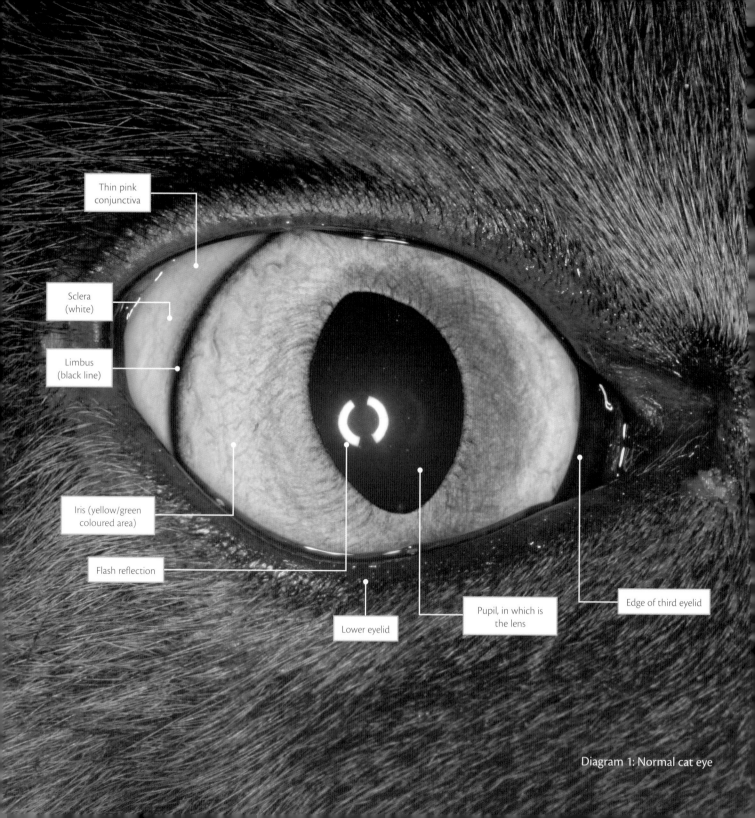

Thin pink conjunctiva

Sclera (white)

Limbus (black line)

Iris (yellow/green coloured area)

Flash reflection

Lower eyelid

Pupil, in which is the lens

Edge of third eyelid

Diagram 1: Normal cat eye

What are the names and functions of the different parts of the eyes?

This section is included for people who are interested in understanding the descriptive terms used throughout the text. Anatomy terms are included, along with the basic function of the various parts of the eye. It may be useful to refer back to this section later as needed.

Eyelids – these protect the eye by blinking, they assist in spreading the tear film evenly across the cornea and they produce part of the tear film.

Third eyelid – also called the nictitating membrane or haw, this structure evenly spreads the tear film and removes debris, and it contains a gland which makes part of the tear film.

Conjunctiva – this pink-coloured thin mucous membrane lines the inside of the upper and lower eyelids and the periphery of the globe. It protects the cornea from drying out, and allows the eyelids to be mobile. It contains blood vessels which provide nutrition to, and remove waste products from, the eye. It also contains lymph tissue for defence against micro-organisms and foreign substances, nerves, and cells which contribute to the tear film.

Tear film – a moist layer present on the surface of the cornea and conjunctiva which is essential to the health of the front surface of the eye. It smoothes out any irregularities on the cornea allowing for sharp vision, it provides nutrition and oxygen to the cornea and thus helps it to stay transparent; it removes debris and foreign material from the front surface of the eye and contains immunoglobulins (antibodies) which help to protect against infections.

Cornea – this is the clear transparent tough outer part of the eye (the outer 'window') which together with the sclera maintains the shape of the eye, provides support for the structures contained within it, and transmits light into the eye.

Sclera – this is a continuation of the cornea and is the white of the eye. This tough outer layer protects the contents of the eye and provides its shape.

Limbus – this appears as a black line and is the junction between the cornea and the sclera.

Anterior chamber – this is the space within the eye between the cornea at the front and the iris at the back, and it contains clear aqueous humour.

Posterior chamber – this term is often used incorrectly to describe the chamber at the back of the eye, which is actually the vitreous chamber containing vitreous (see below). The posterior chamber however is actually the small space behind the back of the iris and the front of the lens. It is a very important area involved in the circulation of the aqueous humour which it contains.

Aqueous humour – this transparent fluid fills the anterior and posterior chamber. It is made by the ciliary body and drained through the iridocorneal (drainage) angle. It is responsible for providing essential nutrition and oxygen to the delicate internal structures of the eye and it absorbs waste products.

Iris – the coloured part of the eye. This structure provides control over the amount of light entering the eye with iris movement by constriction (pupil getting smaller) or dilation (pupil getting larger). In bright light, the pupil constricts to allow less light to enter the eye which protects the sensitive retina, and in low light the pupil dilates to allow more light to enter the eye.

Pupil – this is not a structure but is actually a space in the iris. In the cat, a constricted pupil is slit-shaped, but a dilated pupil is round.

Ciliary body – this structure is located behind the iris. It makes the aqueous humour, provides a barrier from the body's blood supply to protect the eye and provides ciliary zonules which attach to the lens and hold it in place.

Choroid – a layer of blood vessels between the sclera and retina, which also contains the tapetum. This structure serves the retina by providing nutrition and removing waste products.

Tapetum – a layer within the choroid and underneath the retina which acts like a mirror, affording animals better night vision. Light which is not absorbed by the retina passes through to the tapetum, where it is reflected back onto the retina for a second chance at being absorbed by the rods and cones.

Iridocorneal angle (drainage angle) – this is the space at the base of the iris through which aqueous fluid exits the eye. It contains pectinate ligaments with spaces in-between them.

Lens – the lens is a transparent spherical structure which changes thickness to allow an animal to focus on objects. In cats, the thickness of the lens does not alter as much as it does in people, but it still has a very important function in focusing light rays onto the retina.

Zonules – these fine hair-like structures grow from the ciliary body and attach to the lens, keeping it in place.

Retina – this important layer lies at the back of the eye. It contains the rods and cones which are essential for vision. These change light energy into chemical energy and then into electrical energy which is then transmitted through the optic nerve. The optic nerve leaves the back of the eye to travel to the brain where the information it carries is interpreted as vision and light.

Vitreous – transparent gel which fills the main part of the eye, where it transmits light, supports the retina and helps maintain the shape of the eye.

Optic nerve – the nerve endings of the retina converge at the back of the eye to make the optic nerve, and the impulses generated by light and vision are transmitted through the optic nerve to the brain.

Why is my cat blind?

There are many reasons that your cat may now be blind, or severely visually impaired. The most common reasons are listed below. Some cats are born blind, and know no different. Others were normally sighted, but through injury or disease become blind later. The onset of blindness can be very sudden – literally overnight in cats with retinal detachment due to hypertension (high blood pressure) or very gradual, for example in cats with chronic uveitis (long-standing inflammation inside the eye). Cats which are suddenly blind will be more obviously affected by the change than those in which blindness progresses gradually. This is because the change is more sudden to them. The learning curve is sharp in these circumstances, but it is important not to under-estimate your cat. Their ability to adapt to such changes can fill us with feelings of admiration and pride. Cats which slowly become blind can fool you into thinking they can still see beyond the time that your veterinarian tells you that there is no vision at all. They can show very convincing signs of seeing, but in some cases all tests have proven that there is no sight whatsoever. Even cats which have had both eyes removed and therefore positively cannot see, can give an owner a feeling that they retain some visual perception. This is because they learn to cope with their new circumstances using their great memory. They are greatly aided by their amazing instincts, and by features such as their super-sensitive whiskers. This is discussed later.

What causes blindness in cats?

There are many causes of blindness in cats. The cause cannot always be determined despite yours and your vets every effort, but should be investigated every time to ensure the best for your cat.

The most common causes of blindness in cats are discussed below and there are accompanying photographs to illustrate some of the conditions.

1. Hypertension (high blood pressure)

Just as people can suffer from hypertension, older cats can too. They may have high blood pressure because of another health condition, or it may arise spontaneously. Hypertension causes damage to blood vessels which can result in retinal detachment, with or without bleeding into the eye. The early signs can be seen by your vet when they examine the retina allowing a

Right: Hypertension – both pupils are dilated, but the right eye is full of blood. The retina of the left eye can be seen and there are signs of impending retinal detachment due to high blood pressure. However with immediate treatment, vision can be maintained.

diagnosis of hypertension to be made. The diagnosis can be confirmed by measuring your cat's blood pressure. Measuring blood pressure is a routine procedure and cats tolerate it really well. It is important to note that not all cats with hypertension have eye problems at the time of diagnosis.

Signs of hypertension visible to owners include sudden blindness, dilated pupils or blood within one or both eyes. If hypertension is diagnosed, anti-hypertensive therapy (medication to lower the blood pressure) can be prescribed. Anti-hypertensive treatments lower blood pressure and prevent further damage to the eyes (and other organs) which can result as a consequence of high blood pressure. Commonly used medications include amlodipine (trade name Istin in the UK) and benazepril (trade name Fortekor in the UK). Following treatment it is possible for the cat to regain some vision, but this depends on various factors – for example the length of time the retina is detached. If vision is restored, it is usually poor, and all sight may gradually be

lost. If a cause of the high blood pressure, such as an overactive thyroid gland (hyperthyroidism) or kidney problems (chronic renal failure) can be identified, these conditions need specific treatment with medications.

2. Cataracts

A cataract is an opacity in the lens or in its surrounding membrane. Just as people can develop cataracts, so too can your cat. They are not as common in cats as they are in people or dogs. They most often occur as a result of a severe injury or trauma to the eye damaging the nutrition or integrity of the lens. Other common causes are secondary to uveitis or glaucoma (both of these conditions are described below). If a significant cataract develops in both eyes, your cat will be blind. The cataracts can appear white or grey and can be seen behind the iris. An eye with a cataract loses the glow that normal cat's eyes have in the dark, as there is no longer a clear view through to the tapetum which is the reflective structure lying at the back of the eye behind the

retina. There is a surgical procedure to remove cataracts called phacoemulsification which is used in people, and this procedure is now widely performed on animals too at specialist centres. It has its risks and is expensive, but in the right cases it has a high success rate and is a marvellous opportunity to restore sight. Unfortunately not every eye is suitable for this procedure. Uveitis and retinal detachment are both important contraindications for this surgery – in other words, phacoemulsification surgery can make these conditions worse. Your veterinary ophthalmologist will be able to tell you whether this treatment is appropriate for your cat. Unfortunately, there is no non-surgical treatment which successfully improves cataracts in animals.

Cataract surgery is discussed in more detail in the section What surgical treatments might be recommended?

3. Trauma

Certain injuries may result in blindness. The most common forms of injury a cat sustains are blunt trauma such as road traffic accidents, or sharp penetrating trauma such as cat claw scratches from another cat, and, unfortunately, gun shot pellets.

Blunt trauma can cause rupture (bursting) of the eye, and this can occur at the back of the eye where it cannot be seen externally. These eyes generally cannot heal themselves and vision is lost. The force may cause retinal detachment, as this delicate membrane is torn from its normal position at the back of the eye. The retina contains the rods and cones we need for vision, and if it is not attached it loses its blood supply and becomes deprived of oxygen. As a result, the sensitive rods

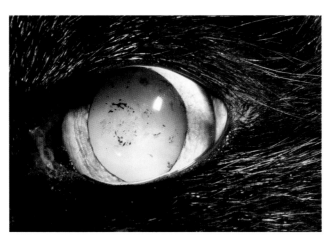

Left: A long-standing cataract (the white structure) with little areas of dark brown pigment on the front of the lens.

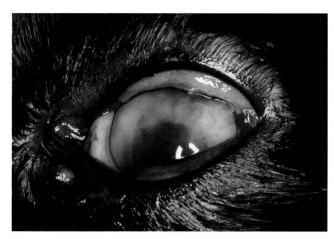

This cat was knocked down by a car. The eye is sore and there is blood in the anterior chamber.

The same eye one week after receiving treatment. Most of the blood has been absorbed and the inflammation is subsiding.

and cones die very quickly and cannot be replaced. Another injury which could occur is lens luxation. Force can cause the lens to move from its normal position, which results in cataract formation or glaucoma.

Sharp penetrating trauma can damage the cornea and if deep enough will rupture the eye. Corneal damage alone can normally be repaired surgically by a veterinary ophthalmologist. However if the sharp claw penetrates a few millimetres deeper and actually tears the membrane surrounding the lens (the lens capsule), the effects are far more serious. Lens material is released into the eye. The body reacts to this lens material as it would to a foreign substance and a severe inflammatory reaction called phacoclastic uveitis occurs. The only way to manage this type of uveitis is to have surgery straight away (within 24 hours) to remove the lens. This is a procedure which needs to be performed by an experienced veterinary ophthalmologist. Unfortunately it is very difficult for an owner and sometimes the initial vet to appreciate the extent of the damage done straight away as the eye is sore and held shut, and the cat hides away. Even on opening the eye, the cornea may be cloudy, the eye may be filled with blood and the pupil may be constricted, hiding the damaged lens. Therefore, disappointingly, it is not unusual to discover that it is too late to save the eye-sight, or even the eye.

Bleeding into the eye can be caused by all kinds of trauma as the eye has a rich blood supply. This can cause several problems. Firstly, it can obscure your vets view into the eye, making it difficult to assess the extent of damage done. Secondly, the blood can block the normal drainage of fluid (aqueous humour) from the eye which can allow the pressure to build up and cause glaucoma. Thirdly, the blood can form a clot which attaches to the retina, and causes it to detach as the clot is absorbed by the body. Fortunately, in some cases it is possible for an eye which is filled with blood to recover with the correct investigation and treatment.

An eye which has sustained trauma can have a variety of appearances, depending on the type of injury and the severity. The eye is likely to be sore causing the cat to shut their eye and hide away. The eye may appear deflated and wrinkled, and the cornea may be white or red. The whole eye may be red if it is filled with blood. It is very important to ask for an emergency consultation at your vets should this happen. Some injuries can be treated, but unfortunately not every eye can be saved if the damage is severe.

4. Glaucoma

Glaucoma is the result of raised pressure inside the eye. Within the eye, intraocular fluid called aqueous humour is constantly being made (by the ciliary body) and drained away (through the iridocorneal angle) at the same rate. This fluid provides essential nutrients to the lens and cornea. An obstruction to the drainage of this fluid causes the volume of fluid to build up as it continues to be produced, and this results in raised pressure. The high pressure places a strain on the delicate retinal nerve cells which gradually die, making vision poorer until it eventually causes blindness.

Glaucoma in cats is most often caused by inflammation, which is called uveitis (see below). Other causes include trauma, bleeding inside the eye or a tumour in the eye.

Even though glaucoma is a painful condition, the cat may display only subtle signs. Usually what is noticed is an enlarged

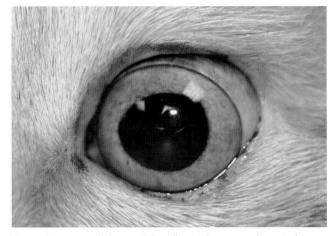

The pupil is an unusual shape and the yellow iris has some red areas in this example of glaucoma.

eye or a dilated pupil, which does not get smaller in response to light. In normal cats, the pupil should constrict (get smaller) in conditions of bright light (eg outside on a sunny day) or when a bright light is shone into the eye. Sometimes, in cats with glaucoma, the white part of the eyes (the sclera) is reddened and the clear cornea may lose its shiny appearance and become duller or a little cloudy (due to oedema).

Your vet will diagnose glaucoma by measuring the intraocular pressure with a small instrument called a tonometer. They will also use this instrument to monitor the response to treatment over time. Eye drops are initially used to try to control the pressure. Commonly used drops include dorzolamide or brinzolamide (trade names Trusopt and Azopt in the UK). These drops reduce the amount of fluid being produced, therefore reducing the pressure build-up. Drops and oral medication may be used to control uveitis, if this is what is causing the glaucoma.

If medication is not successful in managing the glaucoma, some specialists can offer you advanced surgical techniques. Overall these tend not to be successful in the long-term, in which case enucleation (surgical removal of the eye) may be the kindest option for your cat in order to alleviate the pain. It will also mean that the frequent eye drops can stop, allowing your cat to stop having to take medications which aren't working anyway.

5. Uveitis

Uveitis is inflammation of the uveal tract inside the eye, which comprises the iris, the ciliary body and the choroid. These are essentially the vascular or blood-filled areas within the eye.

Causes of uveitis in cats include:

- trauma damaging the lens

- immune-mediated disease causing lymphocytic-plasmacytic uveitis

- infectious agents such as feline infectious peritonitis (FIP), toxoplasmosis, feline immunodeficiency virus (FIV), or feline leukaemia virus (FeLV).

- corneal disease including corneal ulcers can cause sensitivity of the nerves which manifests as uveitis

Signs of uveitis which you might see include pain (squinting of the eye and watery discharge), sensitivity to light, redness of the sclera (which is normally white), cloudiness of the eye (due to oedema) and a change in the colour of the iris.

Your veterinarian is likely to suggest tests to find out the cause of the uveitis. These might include blood and urine tests, x-rays, and ultrasound. For example, cats with FIP may also have fluid

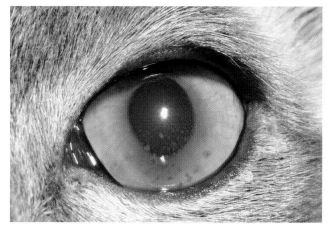

This small kitten had uveitis, and both eyes had lots of white opacities sitting on the back of the cornea due to inflammation inside the eye (uveitis). In this cat, the uveitis was caused by an infection called feline infectious peritonitis (FIP).

in their chest or abdomen which can be seen on an x-ray or ultrasound scan. Aqueous humour samples may be taken from the eye for laboratory analysis. If the underlying cause can be identified, this is treated. Anti-inflammatory medications are used to treat this condition. These are administered orally in pill or liquid form, and as an eye-drop on the eye. Steroid tablets, such as prednisolone, or non-steroidal anti-inflammatory drugs, such as meloxicam (trade name Metacam in the UK) are most commonly used. Common choices of steroid eye drops include prednisolone acetate (trade name Pred forte in the UK), dexamethasone (trade name Maxidex in the UK) or dexamethasone with antibiotics neomycin and polymyxin B (trade name Maxitrol in the UK). Drops to dilate the pupils such as atropine or tropicamide (trade name Mydriacyl in the UK) are very useful to alleviate pain, and to stop the inflamed iris from sticking to the lens which would otherwise be permanent and lead to future problems. Atropine does often cause cats to salivate and froth at the mouth. This does not mean that they are having a bad reaction to the drug – it simply means that the tear duct is working well! The tear duct allows the atropine drop in the eye to drain into the nose and mouth, where it has a bitter taste and causes salivation for a couple of minutes! Therefore it is useful to provide a drink and some tasty food to use up the saliva, but do not worry otherwise. Depending on the cause of uveitis, other treatments such as a course of antibiotics may be prescribed.

Uveitis can be successfully treated in some cases. However other cases only partially respond to treatment and long-term medications are required. In some of these long-standing cases, uveitis can lead to cataracts or glaucoma, both of which cause eventual blindness.

6. Birth defects

Kittens can be born blind. Some are born with one or both eyes which are very small, and these eyes cannot see. In rare cases they are born with no eyes. There are many possible causes for birth defects. They are most often sporadic. In cats, they may result from the mother being given a medication for ringworm called griseofulvin during pregnancy. Affected cats may also have smaller eyelids. If the eyes can be seen they are usually visibly smaller and they may have white corneas.

More often than not, no treatment is required for cats with small eyes. These cats tend to cope very well with their blindness as they have never known any different. The cats are expected to live fulfilling lives of the same length as a normal cat, with some

A close-up of Evie who was born with no eyes, and with very short eyelids.

extra care. They are at increased risk of certain hazards such as road traffic accidents, being chased by other animals etc, and this is discussed later.

Occasionally small eyes must be removed if they are causing problems, or eyelid surgery may be required if entropion is present. Entropion is the name for the condition where the eyelids roll inwards and rub on the surface of the eye which can cause pain and ulcer development.

7. Corneal ulceration

Corneal ulcers are breaks in the outer layer of the cornea, called the epithelium. Possible causes include:

- trauma such as a cat scratch

- underlying disease such as feline herpesvirus infection (FHV, one of the viruses that can cause cat 'flu)

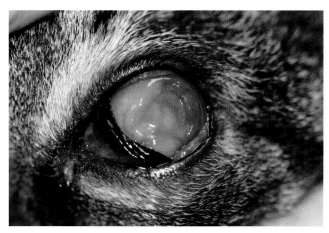

This is a very deep corneal ulcer which needs emergency treatment. This cat responded well to medical treatment, but some cases need surgery and others do not do well with either.

- eyelid abnormalities such as in-turning of the eyelids (entropion) allowing hairs to rub on the cornea

- dry eyes (kerato conjunctivitis sicca)

- an inability to blink because of nerve damage or an enlarged or protruding eye

- infections

Ulcers can be superficial (shallow ulcers involving the outer layer of tissue only – the epithelium) or deep, when they are very serious and can lead to rupture of the globe (eyeball).

Corneal ulcers are very painful. Shallow or superficial ulcers can actually be more painful than deep ulcers, as there are more nerve endings superficially. Thus an ulcer which is very deep can actually be more comfortable than a superficial ulcer, leading to a false sense of security. For this reason, it is important to always attend a follow-up appointment with your vet after the initial diagnosis.

Cats may show signs of pain, such as sleeping more, hiding and eating less. The eye may be closed and may have a watery discharge. The transparent cornea may appear dull or cloudy, and there may be a red appearance as blood vessels attempt to heal the damage.

Your vet will diagnose a corneal ulcer after examination and application of fluorescein dye, which highlights even tiny ulcers. Fluorescein stain is placed onto the eye using a drop or strips which appear orange before they contact the eye, and look green afterwards. The ophthalmologist then examines the eye with a blue light. In normal cats, the green dye does not stick to the surface of the eye and usually spills onto the fur below the eye or flows into the tear duct. Dye in the tear duct drains into the cat's nose so may be swallowed, seen in the mouth or at the nostril a few minutes later! Green fluorescein dye sticks to corneal ulcers highlighting where these are. The ophthalmologist will do other tests to find the cause of the ulcer, including examination of the eyelids, a Schirmer tear test to measure the moisture of the eyes, and use a tonometer to rule out glaucoma. A scraping of surface cells may be taken for examination under a microscope to look at the cells and bacteria involved, in order to provide the most appropriate treatment. A swab may be taken to culture and identify the bacteria or virus involved, and to identify the best antibiotic available to treat it.

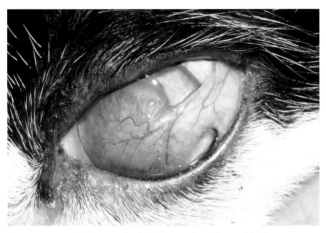

This is an example of an eye which had a very deep ulcer, and had a conjunctival pedicle graft to allow the ulcer to heal. A pink bridge of conjunctiva containing blood vessels is sutured onto the damaged area.

Ulcers may heal uneventfully. However sometimes factors such as infection or dry eyes allow the ulcer to get very deep and even progress to cause rupture of the eye. Medical treatment involves the use of an appropriate antibiotic eye drop which will need to be given frequently. Additional eye drops may be used including:

- artificial tears to provide lubrication to aid healing and to increase comfort.

- mydriatics (drops which dilate the pupil) may be used to control any underlying uveitis.

- anti-collagenases are substances which prevent the action of destructive mechanisms which can occur in deep ulcers. Anti-collagenases are normally present in the serum which

is the liquid component of blood once the red and white cells have been removed. Serum is collected once a sample of blood from your cat has clotted. The blood tube is spun to separate the serum, and this is then used as an eye drop in order to provide natural therapy to combat the problem.

- interferons are naturally produced by the body in order to fight viral infections, and in appropriate cases synthetic interferon eye drops may be prescribed.

Pain relief or antibiotics may be prescribed – for example the non-steroidal anti-inflammatory drug meloxicam (trade name Metacam in the UK). Some cases are more complicated and also require surgical intervention. These procedures include:

- debridement of superficial ulcers: this involves removing the unhealthy epithelium from the edges of the ulcer to encourage it to heal

- a third eyelid flap: this is a procedure where the third eyelid is stitched so that it is covering the eye. Third eyelid flaps help to provide support and a healing environment for the cornea.

- a conjunctival pedicle graft: this is a surgical procedure whereby a section of the cats own conjunctiva is sutured (stitched) into the ulcer to provide blood vessels in order to heal it, and to provide support to the weakened area of cornea.

- a synthetic graft: in this procedure an adjacent piece of cornea or donor cornea (from another cat) may be surgically placed over the ulcer in an attempt to help it to heal.

Most cases heal well after surgery and scarring can be minimal. However, if the injury or infection is too severe, the eye may have to be removed.

8. Feline herpesvirus

Young kittens with feline herpesvirus (FHV, one of the causes of cat flu) can develop severe eye problems at a very young age. There are several different ways in which FHV can manifest in the eye.

Ophthalmia neonatorum is a condition in which FHV allows infection to develop under the fused eyelids of the newly born kitten. The eyelids are swollen and pus may ooze out from them. This can result in development of severe corneal ulcers which can become very deep and even rupture the eye. Treatment involves opening the eyelids and providing antibiotics.

FHV can also cause symblepharon, which is a condition where the pink conjunctiva sticks permanently to the cornea or to itself. Depending on the amount of cornea affected, vision may be obscured. This is not a painful condition. Surgery to remove the conjunctiva from the cornea is often unsuccessful as the conjunctiva sticks to the original site very quickly, and therefore surgery is attempted only in certain selected cases.

FHV can also cause superficial (dendritic or 'tree-branching') or deep (stromal) corneal ulcers. Treatment is as described for corneal ulcers above, and antiviral drugs may also be used. Antiviral eye drops (such as trifluorothymidine) need to be used very frequently to be effective and can cause some ocular irritation. Antiviral tablets such as famciclovir may also be used. Interferon is a substance which the body naturally produces to fight viruses, and this can be given as an eye drop. All antiviral

This Persian cat has a black spot on the cornea of the left eye. This is called a corneal sequestrum and it can occur as a result of infection with feline herpesvirus.

treatment works best in the very early stages of FHV infection, and the treatments are less successful in patients with longer standing viral infections. Lysine is an amino acid which reduces the replication of FHV, and thus may be useful to reduce shedding of the virus and limit future outbreaks. Thus a FHV carrier and in-contact cats may be placed on lysine treatment (available as tablets, capsules or powder) indefinitely. Unfortunately, although safe to administer, this is still considered to be quite a controversial treatment since clinical trials have not always shown it to be beneficial.

FHV most often causes recurrent conjunctivitis (inflammation of the conjunctiva) and keratitis (inflammation of the cornea). Many cases resolve with treatment but unfortunately many affected cats become lifelong carriers of the virus, and subsequent outbreaks in later life are less amenable to antiviral therapy.

Some kittens and adult cats can suffer deep ulcers which can threaten sight, and these require immediate veterinary attention. Some cats develop corneal sequestrum, which is a black devitalised area within the cornea which usually requires surgery to remove it.

Your vet may diagnose FHV by taking swab samples from the eye, by blood tests or in some cases the signs are classical and diagnosis can be made on appearance alone. The cat may or may not have other signs of cat flu such as sneezing.

9. Tumours in the eye

The most common primary tumour in the cats eye is melanoma, and the most common secondary tumour is lymphoma. A primary tumour is one which is in the site where it originally developed whereas a secondary tumour is in a site remote from where it first developed. In other words, a secondary tumour represents spread of the tumour from its original to, often many, new sites. Either form of tumour often causes inflammation,

which leads to uveitis. The inflammation can also result in glaucoma. Both of these effects of the tumour can lead to blindness. Your vet may obtain a biopsy (a sample of tissue) or a needle sample from the abnormal area within the eye to find out what sort of tumour it is, and therefore form an appropriate treatment plan. In more advanced cases, your vet may suggest enucleation (surgical removal of the eye) to try to prevent the spread of the tumour and to get it analysed carefully in a laboratory. Knowledge of the exact tumour type helps to ensure that your cat gets the most appropriate treatment for their condition. Not every tumour is life-threatening, and not all cases require further anti-cancer treatments such as chemotherapy or radiotherapy.

10. Retinal degeneration

This occurs when the sensitive cells which make up the retina die off and can no longer function. In the cat, it can occur as a result of dietary deficiencies, drugs, or inherited disease.

Cats need an amino acid called taurine in their diet, and this is provided in all commercially prepared cat foods. A cat which is fed on dog food or a homemade diet is at risk of becoming taurine deficient. Taurine deficiency causes damage to the retina similar to macular degeneration in people where the retina degenerates causing blindness. Taurine deficiency can also cause a heart problem called dilated cardiomyopathy in cats. No signs may be seen in the cat until blindness becomes obvious, and at this late stage the pupils are normally fully dilated and non-responsive to light. For this reason it is always advisable to feed cats with a good quality cat food, as the damage done to the retina is irreversible.

Left: There was an extensive tumour inside the eye seen as the grey/brown area.

An antibiotic called enrofloxacin (trade name Baytril) has in rare cases of accidental overdose or prolonged treatment caused a retinal degeneration which has resulted in blindness. This blindness can be temporary if the drug is withdrawn quickly but vision can also deteriorate further with time.

Progressive Retinal Atrophy (PRA) is an uncommon disease of cats but may be inherited in Abyssinian, Persian and domestic short-haired cats. There are two different forms – early onset (as early as six weeks has been reported) and middle age (eight to twelve years) onset. There is no treatment for this condition, and it causes total blindness. These cats are born with apparently normal vision but gradually lose their sight. This is usually not noticed until the advanced stages, at which point the pupils are dilated and not responsive to light.

11. Central anoxia/hypoxia (complete or partial lack of oxygen)

Central is a term used to describe the brain, anoxia is the medical term for a lack of oxygen and hypoxia refers to low oxygen levels in the circulation. Central anoxia/hypoxia occurs very rarely as a result of anaesthesia in cats and can cause blindness. Reduced blood supply or reduced oxygen supply to the brain during anaesthesia can cause damage to the area of the brain which is used in seeing. In some cases, the damage is mild and the vision recovers. However in more severe cases vision is permanently lost and sometimes other neurological problems are also present. Affected cats have fixed dilated pupils after recovering from anaesthesia and tend to be quite distressed by their sudden blindness. Fortunately, this complication is uncommon.

What are the signs of blindness in cats?

Signs of blindness vary according to the speed of onset of vision loss. Cats which become suddenly blind may appear disorientated, vocalise a lot and crouch down, appearing unwilling to move. More often, a cat becomes blind more gradually. In this situation, it can be difficult to tell that a cat cannot see when observed in the home environment because they memorise their territory very accurately. If your cat has problems with their vision they may:

- Appear to be quieter and sleep more than normal.

- Occasionally bump into an object that you had newly placed in that position.

- Stop jumping up onto things, and take a long time to jump down.

- Bump into a door that you normally have open but is closed on occasions.

- Start approaching situations more slowly and cautiously, with the head held low to use the whiskers for guidance.

- Walk around a room along the walls rather than straight through it, using the walls for guidance.

There may or may not be visible changes to the eyes.

- The pupils may seem very large, so that less of the coloured iris and more of the black pupil can be seen. In most cases these pupils do not get smaller when exposed to light as they do in normal eyes, but remain large.

- In cases where the retina has thinned, a bright reflective glow can be seen from the back of the eye. The shining structure is called the tapetum which lies at the back of the eye. Most animals have a tapetum to aid them in night vision, and you may see it glowing when you shine your car headlights on animals in the dark. The retina lies on top of the tapetum and dulls it somewhat. Therefore if the retina is thinned or absent due to diseases such as chronic glaucoma or retinal degeneration, the tapetum appears even shinier to us.

- There may be a white appearance inside the eye, which may be a cataract.

- There may be a white appearance on the surface of the eye on (or inside) the cornea.

- The eyes can appear red if they fill with blood, but the redness usually gradually diminishes as the blood is absorbed by the body.

Note the bright reflective sheen in Fluffy's eyes which is the glow of her tapetum. This is much more obvious than is normally the case since Fluffy's retinas have degenerated.

How does a vet diagnose blindness and visual impairment?

If you haven't done so already, it is of crucial importance to bring your cat to your veterinarian for a thorough physical examination and eye examination. Your veterinarian or veterinary ophthalmologist will do their best to discover the reason your cat is blind. They will also offer treatment advice when available, and provide on-going management of the underlying condition. Even when no treatment is available, regular check-ups are likely to be advised. This is because changes can happen over time. In a few cases, the changes can result in secondary problems such as painful glaucoma, which causes suffering and must be

avoided at all costs. If your cat has been found to have systemic hypertension (high blood pressure), ongoing monitoring of blood pressure will be required. This is to ensure that your cat is receiving the correct amount of medication, and is important since these requirements can change with time.

Discuss your concerns with your vet and make sure you get full value from your time in consultation with them. They will not be able to give you accurate advice over the phone or in person without seeing your cat, and it is important that you build up a trusting relationship with them to provide on-going care for your cat even after blindness is permanent. Vets are always keen to make a diagnosis, but owners are keen to hear the prognosis;

in other words, what the diagnosis means for your cat's future. Don't be afraid to ask for the information you require.

If you feel that the relationship you have with your vet is not answering your concerns then you can ask to see another vet within the practice, or look for another practice. Do not feel uncomfortable if you want to do this – your vet should not mind and it is within your rights to choose the vet you feel is best able to look after your cat. It is worthwhile asking if there is anyone in the practice who is particularly interested in eyes. Veterinary surgeons specialising in eye problems (veterinary ophthalmologists) can be contacted by your vet for further advice, if needed. Referral to a veterinary ophthalmologist may be made by your vet, in order to obtain an opinion from a person more familiar with eye problems. If further intricate or complicated techniques will be required, it is best that these are carried out by a specialist.

Your veterinarian or ophthalmologist is likely to ask you the following questions, so it is helpful if you have thought these through before your appointment.

1. How long have you noticed vision problems?

2. Is vision worse in dimly lit conditions, for example, at night?

3. Does your cat appear in good health to you?

4. Have there been any changes to your cats appetite?

5. Has your cat been drinking excessively recently?

6. Have you noticed any weight gain or loss?

7. Has there been any traumatic incident (such as a road traffic accident) that you are aware of?

Sugar is blind and has very dilated pupils and retinal degeneration which has caused her tapetal reflection to be very pronounced.

8. Have you always fed your cat with cat food, or do you make exclusively homemade diets?

9. Has there been any unusual behaviour such as circling, pacing or seizures (fits)?

10. Is your cat on any medications?

11. Has your cat had a general anaesthetic recently?

What does a specialist eye examination involve?

A veterinary ophthalmologist has much experience in dealing with eye conditions. They will receive a letter from your regular vet outlining previous health concerns and current problems with your cat. Using this together with the information obtained from the questions above, he/she can then proceed to examine your cat's eyes in detail. Specialist equipment is used for the examination and to perform diagnostic tests. Your cat will be placed on an examination table and will be gently held there by you, a veterinary technician/nurse or animal care assistant. Most cats are very placid on examination, and it is usually the owners who are more anxious!

Usually the ophthalmologist will first test vision by a menace response (a slightly threatening gesture towards the eye to check for a reaction) and a dazzle reflex (by shining a bright light in the eye which would normally cause the animal to blink or look away). Another test involves allowing small pieces of cotton wool to fall next to your cat, to see if they react to them – cotton wool balls make no sound but the movement can be detected by normal cats and by many cats with poor but some vision. The ophthalmologist also uses a bright light to see if your cat's eyes react to light by constricting the pupil. However, even some blind eyes can retain this reflex.

After careful examination of the areas around the eye and eyelids, much of the examination is conducted in the dark. Using an instrument called an ophthalmoscope, the ophthalmologist will examine the reflection coming from the back of the cat's eyes (called the tapetal reflection, as the tapetum is the bright reflective structure which is in the back of all animal's eyes). By doing this they can see if there are any differences in pupil size and they can see if there are any obstructions to a clear view of the tapetum, such as a cataract in the lens.

The ophthalmologist next uses an instrument called a slit-lamp biomicroscope, through which they can examine the eyelids, conjunctiva, cornea, iris, lens and vitreous with a much magnified view which will reveal even subtle changes.

In order to examine the back of the eye (the fundus, which is made up of the optic nerve and the retina with its blood vessels) a number of instruments and techniques can be used. Most often a head-mounted ophthalmoscope is used with a hand-held condensing lens. Alternatively for a more close-up view, a hand-held ophthalmoscope may be used.

Various tests will be carried out. The Schirmer Tear Test (STT) is used to measure how moist the eyes are and to ensure that there is adequate tear film. The tear film plays an important role in lubricating the eye and providing comfort. A STT involves placing a small strip of indicator paper into both eyes for one minute, with the moisture levels recorded on the strip indicating tear levels of the eye.

Fluorescein stain is placed onto the eye using a drop or strips which appear orange before they contact the eye, and look green afterwards. The ophthalmologist then examines the eye with a blue light. If there are any corneal ulcers they will stain a vivid green, helping the ophthalmologist to make a decision as to how deep or serious the ulcer is. Fluorescein also highlights any leaking from the eye, for example if there has been a penetrating injury to the eye. It is not unusual (and indeed it is a good sign) for you to later notice a drop of this green stain at the nostril or in the mouth, as the dye can travel down the tear duct from the eye to the nose or mouth.

Local anaesthetic drops may be applied to the eye. This will temporarily relieve the surface of the eye of any pain by numbing the nerve endings. The ophthalmologist may use this drop to facilitate further examination, for example, looking behind the third eyelid, or to collect certain samples. For example it can be helpful to take a scraping of surface cornea cells to later examine them under a microscope.

Tonometry is the measurement of intraocular pressure. This test is most often carried out in people by applying a puff of air to the cornea, and people describe it as being unpleasant. We are usually much kinder to our animals! After local anaesthetic is applied, a tonometer is touched lightly onto the surface of the cornea 3-4 times in quick succession. This instrument can measure how firm the eyeball is, and displays a numeric reading. If the pressure is too high, glaucoma can result. If the pressure is too low, there may be uveitis or a leaking corneal wound.

An ultrasound examination may be carried out, especially if the eye is not clear – for example if the cornea is cloudy, the eye is full of blood or if there is a cataract in the lens. Ultrasound is a medical imaging technique that uses high frequency

> **Most cats are very placid on examination, and it is usually the owners who are more anxious!**

sound waves to produce an image of internal body structures. It is similar to echolocation which is used by bats, whales and dolphins. Ultrasound gel is applied to the eye after applying local anaesthetic, and then the probe is gently placed directly onto the cornea. A black, grey and white picture is displayed on the screen and this is then analysed by the ophthalmologist. Ultrasound examination is normally carried out on a conscious patient. Using this technique, conditions such as tumours within the eye, foreign bodies (such as a cat's claw), bleeding and blood clots, retinal detachments and cataracts can be identified and accurately assessed.

Electroretinography (ERG) is a useful test in certain cases of blindness. An ERG is an eye test used to detect abnormal function in the retina, both in the rods and cones. Bright lights trigger an electrical response in the rods and cones, and this can be measured through tiny electrodes which are placed directly onto the eye (after applying local anaesthetic), and under the skin. The test is completely pain-free. However, in order to obtain the most reliable results, cats need heavy sedation or general anaesthesia.

Based on the outcome of the eye examination and above tests, the ophthalmologist may wish to carry out further tests, which may include laboratory tests. Blood tests are useful to investigate a cause for uveitis, or to make sure that your cat is well enough to have an anaesthetic. In other patients a biopsy may be required, which involves removing a small amount of affected tissue and sending it to the laboratory for analysis.

Many of the procedures a veterinary ophthalmologist performs are illustrated on on pages 26-27.

Detailed eye examination

An eye examination should not be stressful for a cat. Except for the first picture, these photos show Jimmy the cat being gently held by Veterinary Nurse Sarah whilst Natasha carries out the eye examination.

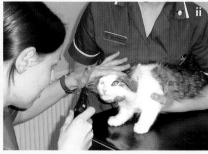

i.   Mog, held by Veterinary Nurse Louise, is having her blood pressure measured in the front leg. Most cats don't mind the procedure. The headphones mean that they can't hear the loud noise of the pulse.

ii.   Testing the pupillary light response (PLR)

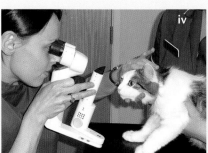

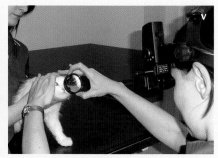

iii.   Distant direct ophthalmoscopy

iv.   Slit-lamp examination

v.   Fundus examination using a head-mounted ophthalmoscope and a hand-held condensing lens.

vi. The Schirmer Tear Test (STT) involves placing strips of paper in the eye for one minute in order to measure the volume of tears (i.e. how moist or dry the eyes are)

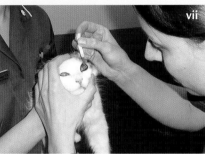

vii. Fluorescein is an orange dye which appears green in the eye. It is very useful for highlighting corneal ulcers and rupture sites.

viii. local anaesthetic drops are placed in the eye to numb the surface of the eye so that the patient can't feel pain. This is useful for certain tests, for example, collecting samples from the cornea.

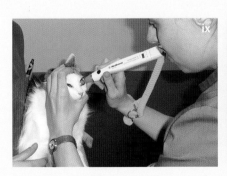

ix. Measurement of the intraocular pressure using a hand-held tonometer called a Tono-Pen.

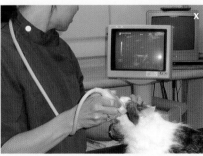

x. Ultrasound examination is carried out by placing the probe directly onto the cornea.

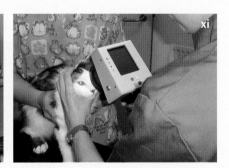

xi. An electroretinogram sometimes requires the patient to be asleep or under general anaesthetic.

What surgical treatments might be recommended?

Some patients require surgery. Unfortunately sometimes the appropriate surgery is enucleation (surgical removal of the eye). However sight-sparing surgery can be offered in some cases, for example phacoemulsification (see below) for some cataract patients.

Enucleation

Surgical removal of the eye is called enucleation, and it is carried out under general anaesthesia. There are a few slight variations in the enucleation techniques performed, but generally speaking the eye is removed and the eyelids are permanently stitched closed. Initially, the appearance after surgery is not very nice as the hair around the eye is shaved and the eyelids are swollen. Occasionally a small amount of blood can ooze from the surgical wound in the early days after surgery, and a drop of blood can even appear at the nose after travelling down the tear duct. Your cat will probably have to wear a buster / Elizabethan collar, to prevent them from scratching their stitches out. Most cats are more concerned about this indignity than about the surgery which was carried out. Remember to do as your veterinary surgeon advises. If you remove the collar prematurely allowing your cat to scratch and possibly remove any stitches, you may be faced with having to put them through another anaesthetic to repair the damage. Of course if your cat really can't eat with a collar on, you can remove it just for mealtimes and for supervised periods on your lap.

Usually the buster collar can be removed after just seven to ten days by which time the surgical area does not bother the cat at

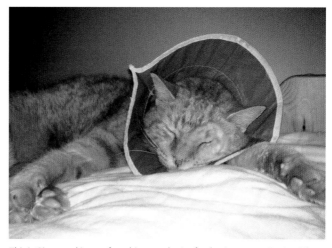

This is Ginger waking up from his anaesthetic after having an enucleation. The buster collar is placed to stop him from scratching at his stitches.

all. Within a period of a few short weeks, the hair grows back and the eyelids heal, by which time the area looks very much better.

Occasionally a procedure called an evisceration with placement of an intraocular prosthesis is carried out. Under general anaesthesia, the eye is opened and the contents are removed. A prosthetic silicone ball (the artificial eye) is placed inside the eye and it is stitched closed. Some people feel that the result is better cosmetically and less traumatic for the cat. However the eye still cannot see, and looks abnormal. You can discuss if your cat is suitable for this procedure with your veterinary ophthalmologist. This procedure is not suitable for certain eyes, for example if there is corneal ulceration, rupture of the eye, tumours in or around the eye or infections within the eye. Also the whole eye is not available for laboratory analysis which is very important for certain conditions such as tumours. Therefore the advice of your veterinary ophthalmologist should be followed.

It can be very distressing to be told that your cat needs to have both eyes removed. This is necessary in eyes which are not responsive to medication and are painful, such as those affected by glaucoma. It is also necessary with certain tumours in order to try to prevent them from spreading elsewhere in the body. It is hard to imagine your pet without those eyes with which you have always engaged and communicated. However they still look just as lovable – as you can see from the photograph of Charlie. Remember that you will not be advised to do this procedure without good reason, and it is unthinkable to allow on-going pain or the threat of further health problems. It is

possible to remove both eyes under the same anaesthetic, and prepare to be surprised by the speed of recovery. If an eye was causing pain before surgery, they will frequently act like a 'new cat' afterwards, being more active and playful than ever before.

Cataract surgery

The technique used to treat cataracts in cats is very similar to the technique used in humans. There is one notable difference however; the cat will always require a general anaesthetic! Through one or two small incisions at the periphery of the cornea which allow the insertion of instruments, the lens can be removed using a procedure called phacoemulsification. A circular tear is made in the thin membrane surrounding the lens (known as the capsular bag). The phacoemulsification

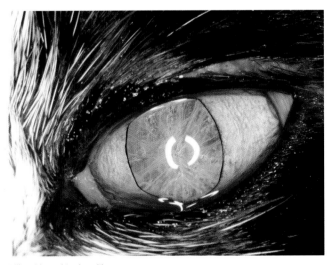

Billy with a white lace-like cataract

Billy the morning after cataract surgery, and there is now a prosthetic lens in the place of the cataractous lens.

probe is inserted through this hole so that it is in contact with the lens. The tip of the probe vibrates with an ultrasonic frequency, which breaks the cataract up into tiny pieces. The small pieces are removed from the eye by the probe at the same time. Where possible, an artificial lens is then inserted. This is injected through the same small incision and unfolds once in the capsular bag where it remains permanently. The artificial lens helps to restore normal sharpness of vision and also helps to reduce the complication of lens cells re-growing. Tiny stitches are placed to repair the corneal incision. Frequent eye drops and much aftercare are required, but this is a very rewarding surgery in the right cases since vision can be greatly improved. Only your veterinary ophthalmologist can decide if an eye is suitable for cataract surgery with a view to restoring sight.

Why is it important to provide permanent identification for my cat?

One of the first things to do when you discover that your cat has problems with their vision is to ensure that they have some form of permanent identification. One of the most useful methods is microchipping. A small microchip is inserted under your cat's skin by your veterinarian. When scanned, this chip reads an individual code, which can be traced to you with a single phone call. Therefore if your cat strays (blind cats are more likely than sighted cats to get lost), and is picked up by an animal authority or brought to the vets, you will be alerted as quickly as possible.

If your cat is already microchipped, make sure that the contact details which you gave at the time of originally placing the microchip are correct and up to date. If you have had any changes, contact the microchip company straight away and let them know. You can provide them with a secondary contact number in case you are away when your cat strays.

Another useful form of identification is a cat collar. Break-away collars with a safety release catch are recommended to ensure that the collar can do your cat no harm. Attach a tag to the collar with information as to your cat's disability ("I am blind" or "I am deaf-blind") so that people know to take extra care and to call you sooner rather than later if they find the cat. Provide at least one, but preferably two phone numbers, and an address if there is room. Also attach a bell to the collar so that you can be more aware of what your cat is up to around the home.

How does a cat with vision in only one eye cope?

Cats with vision in only one eye can behave remarkably normally, so much so that you may be very surprised to learn this about your cat, and visitors may be unaware until you tell them. There may be some slight changes in how they behave and in how they interact with other cats. Many people think that one-eyed animals lose their depth perception – in other words the ability to see the world in three dimensions. Depth perception is important for judging distances, and is used by a cat to jump up and down, and to play or hunt prey. Certainly judging distances becomes more difficult for these cats, but they do adapt very well. They tend to gauge distance by raising and lowering their heads, and sometimes will miss a target. Moving objects are easier for them to judge than static objects, which is why they can still play and hunt remarkably well.

Baby loves relaxing on the windowsill, especially when the sun is shining.

Sybil the blind cat still enjoys the great outdoors and loves sunbathing.

There tends to be a slight change in the behaviour of other cats towards a cat with vision in only one eye. Kittens born with vision in one eye tend to be lower in the pecking order as the other cats can realise their vulnerability and tend to approach them on the blind side or circle around them. They do lose the element of surprise in games as the other cats tend to pounce on them from the blind side. However overall there do not appear to be significant negative effects to their lives.

How does a blind cat cope?

Vision is just one of the five senses that your cat possesses. When vision is impaired, the other senses become sharper as they are used more, and compensate for the loss. Cats' superior senses of smell, hearing and touch are much more developed than ours.

They have a highly sophisticated sense of touch provided by their whiskers – these are specialised hairs which can provide sensory information about the slightest movement in the air. They can use whiskers to navigate by feeling their way, measuring distance and warning them of unseen obstacles. Cats also have sensitive long hairs throughout their coat which provide similar information. Their paw pads are incredibly sensitive. Cats have a much keener sense of smell than we do. They use this to locate food, territorial marking, communicate with pheromones and warn against enemies. Through their hearing they can detect a wide variety of sounds and movements, and they use this sense a lot in hunting. All of these senses can develop even more once they are used more often, enhancing sensations. It is important to be conscious of this when you have chemicals in your home, as these will smell extra-strong to a blind cat. For example, it would be best not to place a plug-in air freshener at cat height as they eliminate regular bursts of highly-pungent smells which your cat could find very unpleasant.

A cat can have a very accurate memory which develops very quickly. Blind cats use this to their advantage by mapping out their territory (house or garden) and thus rapidly familiarising themselves with it. It takes a varying length of time for an animal to learn how to navigate and carry out certain tasks but most learn in a matter of days or even hours.

Routine can help your cat to become accustomed to the lifestyle changes which are inevitable. Try to keep the daily routine as stable as possible as your cat may feel more secure with a predictable routine.

What changes should I make to my blind cat's home?

A cat's home is its sanctuary. It provides security but also with environmental enrichment can provide a stimulating and fun place to be. Blind cats do have some special needs and small changes can help to create a suitable environment for them.

Cats which are suddenly blind often benefit from initial confinement. It is helpful to limit the cat to just one room or area within the home until they are comfortable there, while providing for all of their needs (food and water bowls, litter trays and bed). After a period of adjustment (usually three days is sufficient) you can gradually allow your cat access to more of the home. Each cat is an individual, with some being more out-going and wishing to explore, while others prefer to take it one step at a time.

Where possible within the home, try to keep things familiar.

Ideally, the arrangement of furniture in the home should not be changed. Cats will memorise their home territory and have a map in their head of the layout of familiar places. Moving objects frequently may cause them to bump into things and lose some confidence. Keep the cat's bed, litter tray, water bowl and feeding bowl in the same places. If your cat gets disorientated, place them in a familiar place such as in their bed or at the food bowl so that they can realise where they are and start again. Try to avoid carrying your cat around too much as this may disorientate them, although some individual cats like it and will beg to be picked up.

A litter box should be provided, even if you allow your cat outside. It allows them an opportunity to relieve themselves inside in a desirable and safe place should they feel anxious about venturing outside. It also is a useful point of reference as they will be able to smell it from quite a distance away. Make sure that the litter tray is kept clean. Cats will shun litter trays with odours of other cats or old odours of themselves, in which case undesirable soiling in inappropriate sites within the home may occur. Therefore provide more than one litter tray if you have more than one cat, and place them in discreet but accessible places away from food and water.

Food and water should be provided. Many cats will drink more if their water bowl is placed in a position away from their food bowl. A drinking fountain can be an excellent stimulus for drinking, as many cats are attracted to the noise of the flowing water and the sensation of it on their tongues. Food can be offered ad lib for cats that self-regulate the amount that they eat, or otherwise should be offered in frequent small meals where possible. Remember not to overindulge your animal with extra food because he/she has a disability. Being overweight can cause several other problems such as arthritis, heart disease and diabetes. Your cat is likely to be less active when visually impaired, and therefore food may need to be cut back accordingly. Treats do make a very good training aid in providing encouragement and reassurance, but should be given as part of the daily food allowance, rather than as an extra.

Consider the safety of your home. You may need to 'cat-proof' it somewhat in blocking potential hazards such as fireplaces, window ledges and balconies. Ensure that doors to the outside are kept shut. Check that windows are secure as some blind cats can be very adventurous. It may be best to leave toilet seats down.

Where possible within the home, try to keep things familiar. Minimise any disruption to the normal layout of the home. Changes can be made, and your cat will adapt once they have memorised the area again. Frequent changes are best avoided. Moving home may be required, and this is discussed later.

Some blind cats no longer feel secure jumping up onto things. If your cat has a favourite place such as on a tall sofa or bed, you might consider providing a ramp or a low stool or chair to make the climb more achievable by feel. An example of such ramps can be seen on the website www.cdpets.com.

Initially, your cat may get lost or have an accident such as falling down the stairs. Always pick them up if they look confused and

Fluffy's owner keeps the toilet seat down as she loves climbing on the windowsill, despite being blind.

put them in a familiar place, such as in their bed or at the litter tray, so that they can again get their bearings and re-orientate themselves.

Avoid loud noises which may startle blind cats. This may not always be possible, but you may consider asking children to avoid making sudden loud noises. Consider shutting your cat in another room while using the vacuum cleaner if they don't like the noise.

Blind cats can benefit greatly from environmental enrichment. While they tend to stay more at ground level, cats do love high resting places. Consider providing a stool or shelf where your cat can feel elevated, although they may still help themselves to the couch or your comfy bed! Cats also love private places, and if you can provide a hiding place such as a box, they may enjoy that. A variety of beds can be used to provide different resting places throughout the day and night. Some blind cats will still use scratching posts, and one or more should be provided. If your cat isn't using one, you will need to check that the nails aren't getting too long. If they do, you may need to trim them yourself or have your veterinarian do this for you. Cat gyms can be helpful as these provide a scratching post, a place of elevation, a place to play and a place to rest.

Many cats love vegetation, and it is possible to grow a variety of cat grass in the home. Cats love to sense the outside air, and even if your cat is not allowed outside, it may be beneficial to place a grill in front of an open window so that they can smell and hear the fresh outside air. It is important not to offer your cat potentially poisonous plants to play with. The Feline Advisory Bureau website has a useful list of poisonous plants which you might find helpful: www.fabcats.org/owners/poisons/plants.html

It is best to have patience with your blind cat, and allow them to try to complete certain tasks themselves. For example, let them negotiate flights of stairs without carrying them, as they will learn very quickly how best to perform these tasks. Treats may be needed initially to encourage your cat to ascend or descend steps. While your cat is learning this task, you may need a barrier at the top of the stairs to stop them from falling down.

Cora is blind and regularly gets up and down on her cat activity centre by herself. She loves being in high places.

Blind cats can still perform the most amazing feats. It is not unusual for a young active blind cat to be able to catch and hunt insects and small birds. Hunting does not rely on vision alone, and since the blind cat's other senses are so finely attuned they can be very successful at catching prey.

Above all, your cat's home is enriched by your companionship. Learn to talk to your cat often, using your voice to provide guidance and reassurance. Talk to your cat as you approach so that they know where you are and at what speed you are approaching. With comforting verbal support your cat can feel safe and overcome the new challenges presented to them. Provide lavish praise when manoeuvres are carried out successfully. Give lots of cuddles which will make your cat feel important. Negative reinforcement should not be used as the cat may already be nervous.

Will my blind cat be interested in playing with me?

Your cat may want to sleep more than before. This is fine and your cat is likely to be very happy curled up in a warm fluffy ball. However it is worth taking the time to interact with them and encourage them to play with toys and to do gentle activities, as they may get a lot of enjoyment out of it. If they don't, they will let you know very quickly, in true cat style. A blind cat can give a look of disdain as clearly as a sighted one!! Remember that if your cat did not play with toys before becoming blind, they may not start afterwards. However it is worth spending time to stimulate them as it can really enrich their lives. Cats naturally only play for one minute at a time and then stop, therefore prolonged periods of play are not required. However, all cats are different and certain blind cats will play vigorously for many minutes at a time.

There are toys available which are more suited for blind cats and which provide fun at playtime. Scented toys are available for cats, most notably scented with catnip. Approximately three quarters of cats enjoy catnip, as it gives them a temporary euphoria. Even toys that aren't scented can be made more interesting by application of catnip spray. Dry catnip is also available. Toys which make a noise are very interesting to blind cats as they can track their movement with greater ease. Balls or mice which contain bells, rattles, jingles or squeaks can provide much fun. Homemade toys such as a scrunched up ball of tinfoil or even an avocado stone on a tiled or linoleum floor can provide

Although blind, Evie jumps into every box she finds!

entertainment and allow blind cats to run as they develop extra confidence following such an object. Some cats enjoy a squeaky toy which is attached to elastic and suspended, for example from a handle in the kitchen. They hear the squeak of the toy as they play with it and it cannot disappear as it will always spring back into place. Caution does need to be paid to toys which could be swallowed or which could get tangled causing potential strangulation – such toys should only be allowed at supervised play-time.

There are several suitable toys on the market, such as balls containing bells, catnip impregnated mice, squeaking mice on elastic, mice in a roundabout and toys with a rattle. However noises and smells are not essential, so do not throw away old toys or dismiss toys without these features. Variety is the spice of life!

Evie the blind cat performs a backward flip in a successful bid to catch a passing insect

Is it possible for my blind cat to spend time outdoors?

The outside world can greatly enrich the life of a blind cat. Your cat may be given the option of going outside provided that they have a relatively safe enclosed garden or a run to explore. Some blind cats will not have enough confidence to go outside unless you are there with them. Others are more forward and get great enjoyment out of exploring. A cat harness and lead can be used in the initial stages. Some cats however resist the restraint that this provides.

It is best to supervise blind cats when they are out, in case a loud noise or another hazard frightens them. However with time some blind cats can be allowed unsupervised freedom in an enclosed garden and this is not unfeasible. They can get great enjoyment from sniffing the fresh air along with all of the other interesting smells imperceptible to us. There are so many sounds that they can hear and entertain themselves with. Great fun can be had chasing moving objects (detected by sound and air movements), climbing and exploring the garden furniture, and even chasing and actually catching insects or small prey! Certain precautions should be taken as blind cats cannot easily detect and therefore avoid danger. Waterways such as ponds or swimming pools should be fenced off. Objects that will fall when nosily investigated should be secured into place.

Consider attaching a bell to your shoe when you are in your garden if your cat likes to accompany you, so that your cat can follow your movements around the garden more easily. As was mentioned before, talk to your cat so that they know that you are there. Your cat will appreciate being able to interact with you and know where you are. You could consider putting wind chimes over the door, but this is rarely necessary as they have an excellent instinct for finding their way back inside, and not every day will be windy!

Another excellent idea is to provide a boundary for your cat. It is possible to escape-proof most yards and gardens, making them a safe and enjoyable place to be. Several companies provide such a service, and the following websites are recommended for this purpose:

www.cdpets.com
www.purrfectfence.com
www.fabcats.org/owners/fencing/info.html
www.fabcats.org/owners/fencing/info2.html

By providing boundaries, you can be assured that your cat is protected from straying onto busy roads or from meeting outside animals such as predators or territorial cats. Blind cats find it very difficult to defend themselves from attacking predators or cats. Enclosing your garden with these unobtrusive fences can reduce both your stress and your cat's!

> **It is possible to escape-proof most yards and gardens, making them a safe and enjoyable place to be.**

Seamus in his safe outdoor enclosure enjoying the sunshine, being on a raised surface on his activity centre and loving life in general.

How should I take my blind cat to the veterinary practice?

Always transport your cat in a safe cat box. Escape from a cardboard carrier, poorly constructed or broken cat carrier would be very stressful for a blind cat. It is useful to include bedding from home. If your cat needs to stay at a vet surgery or boarding cattery, consider providing the vets or cattery with some bedding or clothing with familiar smells as the new setting will be a bit off-putting at first. However as your cat will be kept in a confined cage, they very quickly feel secure and in no time explore their new surroundings. Let the nurse or cattery owner know that your cat is blind, so that extra special care can be taken to ensure that they are at ease. At the cattery, your cat may feel more secure in an end cage. Having a strange cat on either side can be off-putting for a blind cat since they are unable to read the visual signals of how friendly or otherwise their neighbours are!

Synthetic feline facial pheromones are available as a spray called 'Feliway'. As discussed in the section about moving home with a blind cat, these pheromones create a sense of calm despite the situation being stressful. A spray or two in an empty cat carrier 20-30 minutes before your departure can relax a blind cat who does not enjoy being transported in a confined cat carrier.

If you are moving home, it is possible to take your cat with you.

What special considerations does a blind cat have when moving home?

Your life cannot grind to a standstill because your cat is blind. If you are moving home, it is possible to take your cat with you. Naturally the cat will be confused initially and have several adjustments to make, but do not underestimate your cat's ability to handle these new challenges. Charlie (pictured opposite) has moved home four times, and has happily explored his new environment every time.

It may be advisable to put your cat in a cattery for the few days immediately prior to and after your move. This will allow you to pack and unpack with less worry and enable you to devote more time to your cat when they do arrive. However this is not always an option and below is some helpful information to make the move as stress-free for your cat as possible.

For the last few days before the move your cat will sense a change as things are packed up and favourite perching places are no longer available. For this reason it may be helpful to get your cat used to spending more time confined to a single room where they can feel secure. If possible, provide additional food, water, litter tray and sleeping facilities in this single room without moving existing supplies from their normal place in the home. It is also useful to not wash their bedding (and perhaps some of your own clothes) for a few days prior to the move. Placing this bedding in the new home provides comforting familiar smells.

The use of natural or synthetic feline facial pheromones within this room may help your cat to feel more calm and relaxed about their confinement. All cats naturally produce secretions called pheromones from glands on their face, and they use this scenting to mark out their territory, an action which is associated with a feeling of calm, well-being and security. It is possible to get some pheromones on a clean dry cloth by rubbing it gently on the side of a cats face, and then rubbing this cloth at cat height around the room. Synthetic pheromones are available as 'Feliway' from your veterinary practice as a plug-in diffuser device or as a spray. The plug-in should be placed in a floor-level electrical socket. Pheromone therapy is very useful in potentially stressful situations such as recent blindness or when a blind cat is moving home.

On the day of the move, make sure that your cat is secure in their allocated room. Put a clear sign on the door to warn the movers not to enter this room, as they are likely to have the front door wide open and your cat may panic and try to escape. Remember that you will need to transport your cat in a safe cat carrier that is escape proof.

Adjusting to a new environment can be easier than we might imagine. Again you might consider using pheromones as discussed above to provide the sensation of familiarity and security in the new home. You will need to initially confine your cat to one room as there may still be the possibility of escape

Charlie, with no eyes, who has moved home four times and has settled in even quicker than his partially sighted companions each time!

through a careless opening of the front door by removal people or well-wishing neighbours. Ensure all windows and doors are locked and escape proof. Be careful that the room you first introduce to your cat has no small hiding places. Popular hiding places include the space behind a washing machine in a utility room, or inside the chimney of a fireplace.

Place your cat in the litter tray a few times and show them where the food and water bowls are. In the initial stages it may be useful to leave a radio or TV on so that they can always get their bearings. Feeding small frequent meals or offering food ad lib helps a cat to feel secure as access to food is always a priority.

It is best not to rush the introduction to the whole house. Moving furniture can confuse a blind cat, therefore it is best to wait until the unpacking is finished to allow a room by room introduction to the new home. Allow your cat to discover the house at their own pace and in their own way. Your cat's spirit of adventure will usually encourage them to investigate every inch of the accessible rooms and in no time your cat will know exactly where everything is.

You need to check that your home is safe. Check for hazards such as poor window latches. You can then set about enriching the new home environment as previously described.

> **Allow your cat to discover the house at their own pace and in their own way.**

How should I care for a deaf and blind cat?

Some cats have the added disadvantage of being deaf as well as blind. It is advisable to put a bell on your cat's collar so that you can find them even though they can't hear you calling. An affected cat's remaining senses become finely attuned and they can lead remarkably happy lives. They can sense movements around them by feeling vibrations. Deaf-blind cats may play and go outside in much the same way as a blind cat.

How will my other pets react to a blind companion?

Despite any friction which may have been present in the household between pets beforehand, the other pets tend to be surprisingly sympathetic and understanding to a newly blind animal. A truce is generally declared. This doesn't mean that they will necessarily become best friends. The sighted cats may ignore a blind cat but generally are not mean to them. There may be an initial adjustment period during which the sighted cat doesn't realise that the blind cat cannot pick up visual clues of aggravation or hostility, but will appear to stare back at them no matter what the circumstances. A blind cat will follow around another companion pet by sound, smell and vibrations. Indeed, it is a good idea to attach a bell to the collars of other animals in the household to help the blind cat know where they are and warn them of an approach in advance. Of course, if the cat has become gradually blind, the changes in relationships between the household pets may have occurred without you noticing them.

Sugar enjoys a rough and tumble play-time with sighted companion Jet.

Sugar gets on very well with the family dog.

Should I get another cat to keep my blind cat company?

While a blind animal may benefit from a companion, it is not necessary to enrich his life with a newcomer to the household. Blind cats may enjoy companionship even though they obviously can't see other pets. However if you do not have other animals, do not feel like you must rush out and take on another pet as therapy for your blind cat. You and your family can be companion enough for your cat. While great enrichment can be provided by a bonded companion, introducing a new cat can be stressful with no guarantee that the two cats will get on well. You may have a problem on your hands if your cat doesn't get on with the newcomer. Cats are not quite sure how to react to a blind cat until they figure out that the other cat can't see. The normal interaction between two strange cats meeting for the first time is to stare at each other. As a consequence, the blind cat may appear over-confident to the sighted cat, and this is not always welcomed! However the blind cat rarely shows signs of hostility, and therefore the sighted cat will hopefully accept the situation for what it is.

What if I'm not coping?

If you are finding it too hard to cope with a cat that is blind but otherwise healthy, you may wish to consider re-homing them. There are many charities and re-homing agencies that would be very sympathetic and understanding, and would be glad to help find a new home in this situation. You may have concerns for your blind cat in a new environment and not want to put them through the re-homing process. The vast majority of cats adapt really well. Remember that the person who takes on your cat will know about their disability already and be well prepared to deal with it.

How can I tell if my blind cat is coping?

Your cat's life has been changed by a means out of your control. Therefore your life has indirectly changed too. It is a shock to be aware that your cat can no longer carry on with life as normal. It is important not to act on any immediate reactions. You need to make your decision over time; your pet deserves this.

You have to remember that vision loss for your pet is not the same as vision loss for you. You will have a worse time coming to terms with the condition and watching your cat adjust than they will have. Animals accept most of what life throws at them. Cats are incredibly adaptable, and usually blindness alone is not a justifiable reason for euthanasia (putting a cat to sleep).

Sometimes blindness may come at a time when other health issues are becoming more unmanageable. In this case if your cat is feeling pain and discomfort that cannot be improved despite our best efforts, it may be time to consider letting your cat go by having them put to sleep. It is valuable to talk to other family members and friends who know both you and your cat as they may have a perspective that is difficult for you to have since you are so emotionally involved.

The bond between you and your cat is very special and you are the most in-tune to your cat's needs. If your cat is suffering from pain, discomfort or distress that cannot be alleviated with medication or nursing care, then you will know that the time is right to end the suffering. Providing euthanasia for our beloved cat at the right time is one of the most important acts that we can do for them, allowing them to rest in peace.

What does euthanasia involve?

For most veterinary surgeons, euthanasia involves giving an overdose injection of a barbiturate anaesthetic agent intravenously, usually into a vein in the front leg. Once the injection is started, the cat will lose consciousness within a few seconds and the heart should stop in less than a minute. Occasionally, the veins of the front leg can be very fragile and difficult to access so alternative injection sites need to be used – these include the kidneys and the liver. In any case, the process should be quick and painless.

Although the majority of cats are put to sleep at a veterinary practice, most vets will be happy to come to an owner's home to do this, if desired.

What happens to my cat's body after they die or are euthanased (put to sleep)?

In general the options will be:

- Burying your cat's body at home

- Asking your vet to arrange cremation of your cat's body. If desired, you can ask for an individual cremation to be performed and for the ashes to be returned to you.

Your vet will be able to discuss these options with you. It is worthwhile considering how you would like your cat to be put to sleep (should the need arise) and what you would like to happen to their body while your cat is still well. This will save you the added distress of these decisions when your cat dies.

Is there support available for me in my grief?

It is normal to grieve when we lose a loved one. Family and friends may be able to help you at this difficult time. It is important to talk about what you are going through. Staff in your veterinary surgery will be able to offer you advice and the details of local support groups if you feel that this would help. Pet bereavement counselling is available. In the UK a pet bereavement service run by the Blue Cross animal charity is available by telephone on 0800 0966606, open from 8.30am to 8.30pm daily. All calls are free and confidential. The PBSS also offers an e-mail support service: pbssmail@bluecross.org.uk

More information on this service is available on: www.bluecross.org.uk/web/site/AboutUs/PetBereavement/ ContactingPBSS.asp

What about my other cat/s – are they likely to grieve?

Yes, it is possible. As with people, cats can show grief at the loss of a companion. The behaviour of a cat following the loss of a house-mate is very variable and unpredictable. Some cats seem completely unaffected by the loss, some appear happier once they are on their own whilst others may show signs of grief such as sleeping less, not eating, appearing to look for their lost companion and vocalising more or losing all interest in life.

This process can affect cats (and other animals) for up to a year following their loss. In most cases, signs of grief will disappear within 6 months. You can help affected cats in the following ways:

- Keep routines in the home the same

- If your cat has lost its appetite then try hand-feeding food that has been slightly warmed (to just below body temperature). Consult your vet if your cat has not eaten for three or more days. A complete loss of appetite can cause a potentially fatal liver disease called hepatic lipidosis.

- Provide reassurance to your cat by spending more time with them, grooming them, talking to them and playing with them.

- Don't immediately get a new cat. Although some cats will crave the company of a new companion, many cats will be more upset and distressed if a new cat is introduced too soon. Many cats prefer to be in single cat households and it is impossible to predict what they will feel about a newcomer. So, if your cat seems happy after the loss of a house-mate, getting another cat is not necessary. If, on the other hand, you are keen to expand the home or feel that your cat is 'lonely' then I would advise waiting for at least a couple of months before considering introducing a new cat.

More information on feline bereavement is available on the Feline Advisory Bureau (FAB) website: www.fabcats.org/owners/ euthanasia/bereavement.html. The FAB also has advice on introducing a new cat which could be helpful once a decision has been made to get another cat: www.fabcats.org/behaviour/ introducing/info.html

Below are five accounts written by owners of blind cats describing their cats and how they get on with living with their disability. Hearing how other blind cats have coped can help to appreciate just how happy and remarkable these cats can be.

Evie

The first account is from the owners of Evie (pictured left). She was born without eyes and with very short eyelids, and was completely blind from birth. She is physically normal in every other way, and has had the good fortune to unite with her caring owners allowing her to lead a very normal life. Her owners have kindly provided us with photographs, which highlight her very busy and happy life!

Shortly after we came back from our Honeymoon in 2003, we decided to go along to the local RSPCA shelter to donate some food and money as they had suddenly received 200 hamsters! While there we foolishly decided to go and have a look and see if the cat department was busy. We didn't need another cat, as we already had two rescue cats. So in we trotted, adamant that we were just looking. Like the finest honed sales person, Ellie, a small one year old tortie was sat in her pen, meowing and pawing at a toy mouse. Liam, being the big softy he is, fell for the local tart in an instant. First he acted all cool and walked past. Ellie however knew that a quick roll around on ones back would melt any man's heart. That was it, the no compromise sales tactics worked, she had a buyer. At this point, the real hard sell began, this was a true BOGOF (buy one get one free) deal, buy the cute tortie and receive a free cute mottled brown cat – one cat, two cats, makes little difference – just one problem – the second cat was BLIND! We were assured that Evie, who was blind from birth, had to be re-homed with Ellie (sighted cat) as she needed her seeing sister as a companion, guide and comfort. Heartstrings tugged a

second time and after some serious discussion with the staff at the rescue centre, we agreed to give both cats a home. For the following week, whilst waiting for our new arrivals, we agonised if we had done the right thing – how would we cope with a blind cat and more to the point how would she cope with us, our house, two new cats and our busy lifestyles?

Evie having a snooze after a hard days playing and hunting!

The day of their arrival came and Mel collected them on a Friday afternoon from the Ark; they looked terrified throughout the 20 minute journey back to Havant and when Mel opened the carrier in the lounge Ellie shot straight under the sofa followed immediately by Evie. They stayed there until late afternoon when Ellie ventured out followed shortly by Evie. By the time Liam returned home that evening Evie had forgotten all about her sister and was busy investigating the house by a process of cautiously moving slowly forward and sniffing from the ground as far as she could reach. Within 2 days she had mapped out the ENTIRE NINE rooms of the house and a week later she was running, not walking, around as if she could see.

Over the next couple of months she became accustomed to us and a real extrovert towards our friends and visitors to the house. All of this, despite at the same time, having a conservatory built, a fireplace fitted, a patio laid and suffering cat flu! She coped and her sighted sister exhibited all the signs of stress you would expect in this situation. In regard to the other cats, Evie didn't have any issues, however they are not sure of her – she has no eyes and certainly no fear!!

We introduced her to the garden a few months after she arrived and once summer came, a little blind cat could be found waiting by the back door to go out into the secured garden. When out she would happily entertain herself with all the plants and furniture but most interesting to her is the wild life. Flies, bees, beetles, daddy long legs and any other insects better watch out. She will catch them in mid flight, and has even done back flips and clipped the wings of birds in mid flight to try and stop them. She may not have eyes but her hearing is something else. However, one afternoon we came out into the garden to find Evie crawling along the fence. She found a trellis half a metre off the ground that would make a perfect ladder and used it. Our Jasmine now has to cope without a trellis!

Evie in the house is like any other cat. She uses the litter tray perfectly and always covers up after herself, even copes when we move it from its usual spot – that includes a completely different room (we don't even have to show her). She has an ear for the cupboard where tuna is kept and can even pick up when you remove a can from said cupboard! If we move furniture she walks around it, not into it first, just around it, even before sensing it with her whiskers. She plays with toy mice and they land under furniture; she will run and duck in time to retrieve them. She jumps up on the sofa and crawls along, and then jumps back down. When we have a meal it is naturally essential that she comes to investigate – so mid meal a cat jumps up on the table, much to Liam's annoyance. A toy that has not moved will suddenly be pounced upon without a paw having been misplaced in the process. Yet the best of all is her drug addiction, Catnip is the crack of Evie world and the things she does to get to the catnip need to be seen to be believed.

Evie is a wonder cat and we are so glad that we got her. If there is ever evidence that a sixth sense exists, this cat has it.

Liam and Melanie

She has an ear for the cupboard where tuna is kept and can even pick up when you remove a can from said cupboard!

Ginger

This is an account from an owner of an older cat called Ginger (pictured right) who contracted an infection called Toxoplasmosis. While the infection was controlled with antibiotics, it caused uveitis, which led to glaucoma in one eye which had to be removed. The other eye lost its sight more slowly, allowing him to gradually adapt.

Ginger came to us in 2001, when we moved into our new house. He was living in the area as a stray, some neighbours fed him from time to time with leftovers from ready meals, so his teeth were in bad shape. One of his canines was missing and he had gingivitis.

We fell in love with this big Ginger and he decided to move in. He is an only child.

He was diagnosed with uveitis when he was having an operation to remove an abscess in his left upper jaw; he was prescribed Maxitrol eye drops which did nothing for him. Shortly after his left eye became cloudy, a blood test showed he had Toxoplasmosis and he was on antibiotic tablets for almost two years. He was often in pain and slept a lot.

By chance (his usual vet was on holiday) he was seen by another vet who put him on a different steroid eye drop called Pred forte and this did the trick. He became his old self again and we could even stop the antibiotics.

In the last year he developed glaucoma, his lens was detaching and he had a corneal ulcer. [Note from Natasha – glaucoma results from a build-up of fluid within the eye, and this increased pressure can cause the lens to be loosened from its normal attachment points, the lens zonules]. Last Christmas he seemed to get worse, and his vet recommended enucleation of the bad eye.

But quite some time before that, I got the impression that he was also losing sight in his good eye. He was slow to focus, so he couldn't see things that moved fast like a hand or another cat. The pupil was more or less constantly dilated. He also was and still is much more vocal, he calls when he comes into a room, and he is easily frightened or startled although this has improved since the operation to remove the eye.

He likes playing with one of his humans, a rope or a feather on a stick coming out of a tube or a tunnel are his favourites. When playing he relies mostly on his hearing.

He goes outside into the garden and into our neighbours' gardens, but he is denied access to the front and the street. I do not always supervise, but I try to keep an eye on him and he usually does not venture far.

One day about a year ago we saw him on the fence slightly disorientated, he could not see where it was safe for him to jump down, so my husband made him a catwalk up and along the back fence. There he sits every morning and waits for the sun to come out.

Since losing sight and therefore feeling vulnerable he has started to sing to warn other cats or maybe to give himself courage, so as soon as he gets a whiff of something strange he sings (very annoying for the poor neighbours I assume).

> **He likes playing with one of his humans, a rope or a feather on a stick coming out of a tube or a tunnel are his favourites.**

We do not find it difficult to deal with his blindness, he finds his way around the house and the garden with ease and now the bad eye is out, he seems a lot happier and more self confident.

The only real problem for us was how to let him go outside and decrease the risk of an accident or an injury or even a fight with the territorial tomcat.

I think it would be a lot more difficult to deal with if Ginger was a young cat, but he is a senior and accepts to stay indoors during the night. Even during most of the day he sleeps on the upper bunk bed.

Euthanasia has never been considered and it won't be as long as he has a good quality of life.

There are a number of small inconveniences for us. For example, we never go on holiday together and we never leave him alone for more than a few hours. But he gives us a lot back; and he is much more affectionate than he used to be when he was younger.

Anette

Fluffy

Fluffy (above) developed blindness at a very young age, due to retinal degeneration *of unknown cause. Her littermate was completely unaffected. Apart from occasional bouts of cystitis, Fluffy leads a very happy life in a multi-cat household.*

My blind cat is called Fluffy. She is a semi longhaired black, tan and white cat of about two and a half years. She was a wild kitten that I rescued, with her sister, from a house that was being gutted. They were about 5 weeks old and not used to eating from a dish. She was always easier to handle than her sister and

is now a fully tame cat with me but is afraid of strangers. She likes to sit on my knee, be petted and carried around. Her sister never got this tame.

It took me several months to realise that she was blind as she can go around the house and knows where all the doors are and does not collide with anything that is in its normal place. If I leave something in a different place she will run headlong into it giving herself a fright. Initially I thought she was retarded as she did not have the same aggressive attitude to new cats or dogs (I rescue many animals). While the other cats would growl at a new cat she would walk up to it and might even collide with it. She never shows any aggression or gets into fights. If a cat attacks her she never retaliates. New cats never like her initially as she walks into them which frightens them but after a while she never or rarely collides with them. I don't know if they get out of her way or if she knows their smell and avoids them. She is a glutton for food and is always first to the dish with her head in the centre making it difficult for the others to eat, and she is a little overweight!

When I am working on the computer she gets onto a nest of tables and from that onto the computer table and either onto my knee or onto the top of the computer and then meows for me to lift her down. She would not jump from the top of the computer to the ground, it is too far. She does not usually sit on my knee for any length of time. She jumps onto the floor, gets back onto the nest of tables and repeats the exercise over and over which is very annoying when I am trying to work! As I was writing this I wondered why she was not climbing on the table and then realised I had left a big bag in front of the low tables so she was blocked. When I removed it she started her usual routine. It takes her a while to adjust to any changes.

When she is on a height like a table she will feel for the edge with her paw and eventually climb up. She will jump down from the height of a table but could not jump up that high. She can only jump up if she can feel with her paw to assess the height before she jumps.

She has always used the litter tray but very occasionally stands in the litter but does her business outside the tray. She has no problem finding the water bowl.

She is bad at grooming herself and I often cut out matts. In the bathroom she jumps onto the toilet seat then onto the cistern and then onto the window sill. She will jump from there onto the ground. In the sitting room she jumps onto the chair and climbs the back of the chair onto the window sill. She usually gets down by climbing down the back of the chair (often half falling) onto the seat and jumping onto the floor.

She seems normal going around the house (she never goes outside) except that she doesn't play with the others. Occasionally she tries playing with a toy. She hits it with her paw and smells around the floor to try to find it to hit it again. This is not a frequent occurrence however. I've seen her watching a butterfly on the window and trying to catch a fly on the window a few times. Maybe she can hear the flies. She seems to be very happy and content.

Linda

Seamus

Seamus (pictured right) is a three-year-old cat who was adopted by the veterinary technician (nurse) who cared for him when he was in an animal shelter. He was probably left there because his eyes were abnormal. They were both abnormally small (referred to as microphthalmos) and they contained cataracts. One eye was blind and the other was severely visually impaired. Because his eyes were so small, they didn't completely fill the sockets. This allowed his eyelids to roll inwards (called entropion) allowing the hairs to rub on the cornea which is a very painful condition. Seamus was indeed in a sorry state when he was brought to the animal shelter but his life was about to change...

I met Seamus while working at a veterinary eye practice here in Northern California. A local animal shelter had received him as a stray; he was about 6 months old and had obvious problems with his eyes. The shelter manager brought him to the eye practice for an evaluation, to see if he could be put up for adoption with his eye condition. (His name at the time was "See-More", named by the shelter volunteers.) He was an amazingly confident young cat, despite his poor vision; he hopped out of the cat carrier and proceeded to boldly inspect the room by sniffing loudly. His eye exam revealed a complete cataract in one eye and an almost complete cataract in the other, as well as bilateral microphthalmia (abnormally small eyes) which had led to entropion (eyelids rolling inwards). He did have some vision in the one eye. Obviously as he was born with the cataracts, he had never known what "normal" was. I was really struck by how comfortable he was with his lack of vision, and how willing he

was to explore new surroundings. The ophthalmologist I worked for agreed to admit him for bilateral entropion correction and also offered to neuter him.

He only stayed that night and most of the next day at our practice, and the ophthalmologist I worked with did the entropion surgery, and neutered him. The plan was to return him to the shelter to be put up for adoption. However in the time he was with us I completely fell in love with him. At the time, I only had one cat, an 18-year-old calico. Two months before, I had lost a 6-year-old cat who had also been visually impaired since birth. After her death I was reluctant to get another cat for fear of stressing out my older cat, but I just couldn't resist "See-More". I adopted him and re-named him Seamus, and to my relief my older cat seemed to accept him, or at least she allowed him to be around her! He also got along well with my dog Kirby. It wasn't long before Seamus had the layout of the house memorized, and could dash from one room to the other with confidence.

Two months later, my older cat had to be euthanized (put to sleep). I was so grateful to have Seamus there when I returned home from the emergency vet; the house would have felt so lonely if it hadn't been for him.

Two months after that, another visually impaired kitten was brought into the eye practice for evaluation – a 4-month-old with an adherent leukoma (white opacities) on one cornea. Like Seamus, he was incredibly outgoing and friendly, and I ended up adopting him as a playmate for Seamus. I named the new arrival Finnegan. He and Seamus became great friends almost immediately.

Seamus and Finn LOVE my cat enclosure. It is up against the back of my house, and the cats jump up onto a window perch and go through a pet door in a window screen to get into it. They have to jump down three shelves, like steps, to get to the ground. The first time Seamus went out, I brought him into the enclosure through the "human" door that leads into the enclosure from the back yard. I let him sniff around on the ground, then lifted him onto the bottom shelf and let him inspect that. He had enough vision to then jump down by himself. Soon he jumped back up, and soon after that he discovered the next highest shelf. When he discovered the third (highest) shelf, I held the pet door leading into the house open, and helped him go through onto the window perch inside the house. When he turned around to come back out, I opened the cat door just enough that he had to push his head against it to come back out. That's really all it took – because he had some vision, I really didn't worry about him falling off of a shelf. I've seen Seamus run through the house at full speed, leap onto the window perch and go out the pet door into the enclosure without putting a foot wrong. The only thing that he seems insecure about is sudden loud noises; he will bolt for cover immediately.

My cats are really happy and I never once considered euthanasia. I often saw owners that did consider having their pets who lost their vision put to sleep, and had to counsel them about the fact that dogs and cats don't waste time feeling sorry for themselves the way humans do. These owners thought that their pet would be "sad that they couldn't see anymore", when the truth is that with a little bit of extra care these animals can lead very happy and fulfilling lives, just like my cats!

Karen

Sugar

I actually first saw Sugar (pictured right) as her owners posted an incredible video of her playing on you-tube (an internet site onto which people place home videos for viewing) and was amazed to see her playing vigorously with a mouse for four minutes in perfect bliss! Having contacted the owners, they told me the following story.

We rescued Sugar from a family divorce situation. She was part of a litter of kittens all of which (except her) were killed by the mother. She was taken away from her mother and bottle fed for 5-6 weeks.

Sugar does not know she is blind because she has never seen anything. She confuses my other two cats because she cannot communicate well with them by looking at them, but they co-exist very well. Kippy the older cat doesn't interact much with her but the younger cat (Jet) adores her and they chase each other around very often, playing very vigorously on occasions. Sugar typically plays for 2-20 minutes, it depends on if anything distracts her. She loves crumpled up paper, toy mice, string etc. She enjoys running but knows it can be dangerous so she runs behind me or her buddy Jet. She has nightly games with Jet of hide and seek, pounce and kick and also football with crumpled paper. She also loves things that she shouldn't, like tape! Fetch is her favourite game.

She does everything the other cats can do with the exception of jumping up on certain things or jumping down. She will happily jump if she can reach it with her paws. She is very trusting of me and knows she is safest in our arms and lays there like a rag doll. Her whiskers and her ear hair have grown very long to compensate. She also explores with her tail down to help feel behind her. She can keep track of many things or people at once. She "scans" the room top to bottom and side to side in order to pin point where sounds are coming from.

Sugar has incredible hearing and can hear an insect crawling on the outside of the window! She has caught MANY flies in mid air! She adores catnip. She crawled up the long coats in the closet in order to get to the catnip on the top shelf. She can also untie shoelaces in seconds. Her record is five in one day!

Sugar always finds the enclosed litter box even if we move it and is very good at TRYING to cover things up. Bless her heart she scratches everywhere, the side of the box, the top of the box, outside the box, three feet away from the box sometimes! It takes her longer to scratch around than the actual duty itself.

She loves to explore outside and follows me everywhere. She is very cautious outside as we have a lot of birds and traffic by our house. When unsure or exploring the yard, she taps her paw in front of her like a blind person using a stick. We have tried using a harness on her, as we use them on my other two cats. However she really resists so we no longer try, she explores quite safely anyway.

Sugar is a very content cat and leads a happy fulfilled life. Her blindness is hardly a handicap, she is not troubled by it. She gives us so much pleasure, we would recommend that anyone take the time to care for a blind cat, it has been so very rewarding for us.

Lynne & Dean

There are several websites with useful information on the care of blind cats and on specific causes of blindness. There are also chatrooms and forums for people with disabled pets to discuss the disability and ask for advice. It can be very comforting to know that you are not alone, and that there are other people going through the same thing who can sympathise with you and offer advice. Remember that all advice you receive is the opinion of the individual offering it, and you must think carefully before you accept the advice of people who don't know you, your cat or your situation.

General cat advice

The Feline Advisory Bureau: www.fabcats.org

The Blue Cross: www.bluecross.org.uk/web/site/home/home.asp

Cats Protection: www.cats.org.uk/

The Royal Society for the Prevention of Cruelty to Animals: www.rspca.org.uk/

The Cat Group: www.fabcats.org/cat_group/index.html

American Association of Feline Practitioners: www.catvets.com

General information on care of blind cats:

www.cats.org.uk/catcare/leaflets/VET09-Blindcats.pdf is a guide produced by the Cats Protection charity providing a concise and useful leaflet.

http://groups.yahoo.com/group/Handicats/ This is a forum for owners of cats with handicaps, and there are some discussions on blind cats which you can join.

http://blindcatrescue.com/ is a website of a rescue centre and sanctuary for blind cats in North Carolina.

www.disabledanimalsclub.co.uk/1.html is the official website for the Disabled Animals Club

Information on fencing gardens and making cat enclosures:

www.cdpets.com – this company provide enclosures to keep your cat safe when outdoors. They also make ramps which would be very useful to allow the more hesitant blind cats to still enjoy their perches on windowsills, your bed etc.

www.purrfectfence.com/ is a website of a company providing cat enclosures. These allow your blind cat to be happy and safe outdoors, and the company operates in both the UK and the USA.

www.fabcats.org/owners/fencing/info.html – information from the Feline Advisory Bureau on fencing gardens

www.fabcats.org/owners/fencing/info2.html – more information from the Feline Advisory Bureau on fencing gardens

Bereavement support

www.bluecross.org.uk/web/site/AboutUs/PetBereavement/ContactingPBSS.asp

www.fabcats.org/owners/euthanasia/bereavement.html

Miscellaneous information

www.fabcats.org/behaviour/other/catnip.html for more information on catnip and its effects on cats

www.fabcats.org/owners/poisons/plants.html for more information on poisonous plants in the home and garden

www.fabcats.org/behaviour/introducing/info.html for more information on introducing a new cat to the household

www.fabcats.org/owners/moving/info.html for more information on moving house with a cat

Further reading

For those interested in a deeper understanding of eye conditions and treatment, a very useful book describes veterinary ophthalmology In a practical and user-friendly way. It is actually written for veterinary nurses and technicians, but with its well-illustrated text, all interested people can learn from the book.

Veterinary Ophthalmology. A manual for nurses and technicians. Author: Sally Turner. Publisher: Elsevier. 2005. ISBN 0750688416

Glossary of terms used by vets

Anatomical terms are described in 'What are the names and functions of the different parts of the eyes?'

Term	Definition
Anaesthesia	Providing a state of unconsciousness, muscle relaxation and loss of pain sensation using certain drugs (usually a combination of intravenously and by gas inhalation).
Anterior chamber	This is the space within the eye between the cornea at the front and the iris at the back, and it contains clear aqueous humour.
Antiviral	A drug which is effective against a virus. Antiviral agents may work in one or more ways for example: ■ Enhancing the cat's immune function and their ability to fight the infection themselves ■ Making tissue cells more resistant to infection with a virus ■ Reducing a virus' ability to replicate (multiply) in the body
Aqueous humour	This transparent fluid fills the anterior and posterior chamber. It is made by the ciliary body and drained through the iridocorneal angle. It is responsible for providing essential nutrition and oxygen to the delicate internal structures of the eye and it absorbs waste products.
Biopsy	Collection and laboratory analysis of a sample of tissue e.g. eyelid biopsy.
Cataract	An opacity of the lens or the membrane surrounding this.
Choroid	This is a layer of blood vessels between the sclera and retina, which also contains the tapetum. This structure serves the retina by providing nutrition and removing waste products.
Chronic renal failure	Inadequate kidney function which has been present for at least two weeks. This is considered to be a progressive condition – it will get worse with time – although the speed of progression is variable.
Ciliary body	This structure is located behind the iris. It makes the aqueous humour, provides a barrier from the body's blood supply to protect the eye and provides ciliary zonules which attach to the lens and hold it in place.
Clinical examination	Examination of body systems by a veterinary surgeon or nurse. Typically this includes listening to the chest, opening the mouth and feeling the tummy.

Term	Definition
Clinical signs	The term used to describe what we would call our 'symptoms' if we were the cat e.g. bumping into objects.
Conjunctiva	This pink-coloured thin mucous membrane lines the inside of the upper and lower eyelids and the periphery of the globe. It protects the cornea from drying out, and allows the eyelids to be mobile. It contains blood vessels which provide nutrition to, and remove waste products from, the eye. It also contains lymph tissue for defence against micro-organisms and foreign substances, nerves, and cells which contribute to the tear film.
Conjunctivitis	Inflammation of the pink mucous membrane which lines the eyelids and the sclera (the white portion of the eye).
Cornea	This is the clear transparent tough outer part of the eye (the outer 'window') which together with the sclera maintains the shape of the eye, provides support for the structures contained within it, and transmits light into the eye.
Entropion	Turning in of the eyelid or a section of the eyelid, which causes hairs to contact the surface of the eyeball.
Enucleation	Surgical removal of the eyeball.
Euthanasia	Also referred to as 'putting to sleep', this is the term used when a vet ends a cat's life. This is usually done by giving an overdose of barbiturate anaesthetic into a vein in the leg – the cat dies within seconds of the injection being given.
Eyelids	These protect the eye by blinking, they assist in spreading the tear film evenly across the cornea and they produce part of the tear film.
Feline herpesvirus (FHV)	This virus is unique to cats and can cause a wide range of clinical signs including rhinotracheitis (inflammation of the nose and throat). Eye-related syndromes associated with FHV infection include conjunctivitis, keratitis (including superficial or deep corneal ulcers), ophthalmia neonatorum and symblepharon.

Term	Definition
Glaucoma	The term used to describe raised intraocular pressure to a level which is not compatible with the normal functions of the eye, causing damage to the sensitive retina and optic nerve.
History taking	This is the process by which your vet gathers information on your cat and all of its problems (clinical signs).
Hypertension	Cats with systemic hypertension have a persistently elevated systolic blood pressure above that which has been found to be normal in cats (the exact figure varies depending on the technique used to measure blood pressure in cats).
Hyperthyroidism	This is a medical condition which causes an excessive level of thyroid hormone which commonly results in weight loss, excessive hunger and can cause hypertension.
Inflammation	A response of injured or damaged cells which helps to wall off the problem, eliminate infectious substances (for example) and restore healthy tissue. The classic signs of inflammation are: ■ Heat ■ Pain ■ Redness ■ Swelling ■ Loss of function
Inflammatory	Pertaining to inflammation.
Intraocular pressure	The pressure or firmness created within the eyeball by the continued renewal of aqueous humour.
Iridocorneal angle	Also referred to as the drainage angle this is the space at the base of the iris through which aqueous fluid exits the eye. It contains pectinate ligaments with spaces in between them.
Iris	The coloured part of the eye. This structure provides control over the amount of light entering the eye with iris movement by constriction (pupil getting smaller) or dilation (pupil getting larger). In bright light, the pupil constricts to allow less light to enter the eye which protects the sensitive retina, and in low light the pupil dilates to allow more light to enter the eye.

Term	Definition
Keratitis	Inflammation of the cornea, which may or may not be ulcerated.
Lens	The lens is a transparent spherical structure which changes thickness to allow an animal to focus on objects. In cats, the thickness of the lens does not alter as much as it does in people, but it still has a very important function in focusing light rays onto the retina.
Limbus	This appears as a black line and is the junction between the cornea and the sclera.
Oedema	The accumulation of excessive amounts of watery fluid in cells or in spaces between cells. This can lead to puffiness of the area. With relation to the eye, corneal oedema can make the normally clear cornea appear white or grey, while conjunctival oedema is also termed 'chemosis' and can make the pink tissue surrounding the eye appear swollen to the extent that the eye itself may be obscured.
Ophthalmia neonatorum	Conjunctivitis in a newborn animal behind closed eyelids.
Ophthalmologist (Veterinary)	A veterinary surgeon with further education and considerable experience in eye care for animals.
Ophthalmoscope	An instrument used to examine the eyes. Different types of ophthalmoscope are available and have slightly different purposes.
Optic nerve	The nerve endings of the retina converge at the back of the eye to make the optic nerve, and the impulses generated by light and vision are transmitted through the optic nerve to the brain.
Pathologist	A specialist in pathology who is able to diagnose the cause and/or type of disease by examining biopsy samples.
Pathology	The study of disease.
Physical examination	Examination of body systems by a veterinary surgeon or nurse. Typically this includes listening to the chest, opening the mouth and feeling the tummy.

Term	Definition
Posterior chamber	This term is often used incorrectly to describe the chamber at the back of the eye, which is actually the vitreous chamber containing vitreous. The posterior chamber however is actually the small space behind the back of the iris and the front of the lens. It is a very important area involved in the circulation of the aqueous humour which it contains.
Prognosis	A forecast of the likely long-term outlook for a cat with a given condition/s.
Pupil	This is not a structure but is actually a space in the iris. In the cat, a constricted pupil is slit-shaped, but a dilated pupil is round.
Retina	This important layer lies at the back of the eye. It contains the rods and cones which are essential for vision. These change light energy into chemical energy and then into electrical energy which is transmitted through the optic nerve. The optic nerve leaves the back of the eye to travel to the brain where the information it carries is interpreted as vision and light.
Retinal degeneration	This occurs when the sensitive cells which make up the retina die off and can no longer function. In the cat, it can occur as a result of dietary deficiencies, drugs, or inherited disease.
Retinal detachment	Displacement of the innermost, light-sensitive layer which normally lines the back of the eye.
Sclera	This is a continuation of the cornea and is the white of the eye. This tough outer layer protects the contents of the eye and provides its shape.
Sedation	Providing a state of calm and muscle relaxation using drugs. The cat is still conscious but, depending on the drugs used, may appear quite sleepy.
Symblepharon	Abnormal adhesions of the conjunctiva to itself or to the cornea, usually caused by feline herpesvirus or chemical injuries.
Tapetum	This is a layer within the choroid and underneath the retina which acts like a mirror, enabling animals to have better night vision. Light which is not absorbed by the retina passes through to the tapetum, where it is reflected back onto the retina for a second chance at being absorbed by the rods and cones.

Term	Definition
Tear film	A moist layer present on the surface of the cornea and conjunctiva which is essential to the health of the front surface of the eye. It smoothes out any irregularities on the cornea allowing for sharp vision and provides nutrition and oxygen to the cornea and thus helps it to stay transparent. The tear film is important in removing debris and foreign material from the front surface of the eye and contains immunoglobulins (antibodies) which help to protect against infections.
Third eyelid	Also called the nictitating membrane or haw, this structure evenly spreads the tear film and removes debris, and it contains a gland which makes part of the tear film.
Tonometer	An instrument used to measure the intraocular pressure, which is lightly touched onto the surface of the eye to obtain a reading.
Ulcer	An erosion in the skin or epithelial lining of a body tissue. Corneal ulceration can occur and can be superficial (shallow) or deep. Deep corneal ulcers can progress to cause rupture (bursting) of the eyeball.
Uveitis	Inflammation of the iris, choroid, and/or ciliary body inside the eye.
Vitreous	This is the transparent gel which fills the main part of the eye. The vitreous is responsible for transmitting light, supporting the retina and helping to maintain the shape of the eye.
Zonules	These fine hair-like structures grow from the ciliary body and attach to the lens, keeping it in place.